CHIP

D0622029

Some recent books
by
WALTER LOWENFELS

POETRY

Some Deaths

Thou Shalt Not Overkill

Found Poems & Others

EDITOR

Walt Whitman's Civil War

Poets of Today: A New American Anthology

Where is Vietnam? American Poets Respond

In the Time of Revolution: Poems from our Third World

The Writing on the Wall: Protest Poems, Whitman to Today

The Tenderest Lover: Whitman's Erotic Poetry

PROSE

To An Imaginary Daughter

The Life of Fraenkel's Death (WITH HOWARD MCCORD)

Robert Gover's The Portable Walter

The Poetry of My Politics

From
the Belly
of
the Shark

We are in the belly of the shark,
and the question of whether or not
to gut the shark is academic.
It is clearly a question of method.

—HERMINO RIOS

From the Belly of the Shark

A NEW ANTHOLOGY OF NATIVE AMERICANS

Poems by Chicanos, Eskimos, Hawaiians,
Indians, Puerto Ricans in the U.S.A.,
with related poems by others

Edited by WALTER LOWENFELS

with introductions by
DAVID HERNÁNDEZ, CLARENCE MAJOR,
SIMON ORTIZ, RARIHOKWATS,
RICARDO SÁNCHEZ, MADELYN SHULMAN

VINTAGE BOOKS
A Division of Random House/New York

First Vintage Books Edition, July 1973

Published in the United States by Random House, Inc., New York
and simultaneously in Canada
by Random House of Canada Limited, Toronto.

Library of Congress Cataloging in Publication Data

Lowenfels, Walter, 1897–   comp.
From the belly of the shark.

1. American poetry—20th century.
2. United States—Literatures—Translations into English.
I. Title.
[PS586.L68]   811'.5'08   73–262
ISBN 0-394-71836-4 (pbk.)

Manufactured in the United States of America

COVER PHOTO: Courtesy of the Museum of the American Indian.

INDIAN Alta, "Thanksgiving": reprinted by permission of Alta and
Shameless Hussy Press. Robert Bacon, "Mister Scoutmaster": re-
printed by permission of Robert Bacon. Duane Big Eagle, "Bidato":
Copyright © 1971 by Duane Big Eagle. Dolly Bird, "Return to the
Home We Made": from *Akwesasne Notes.* Lew (Short Feathers) Block-
colski, "Museum Exhibition": from *Akwesasne Notes,* Vol. 3, No. 8,
1971. Besmilr Brigham, "North from Tanyana": from *Heaved From the
Earth,* Alfred A. Knopf, Inc. Copyright © 1971 by Besmilr Brigham.
Joseph Bruchac, "Indian Mountain": Copyright © 1971 by Ithaca
House. Gladys Cardiff, "Dragon Skate": reprinted by permission of
Gladys H. Cardiff. Robert J. Conley, "We Wait": reprinted by permis-
sion of Robert J. Conley. Carl Concha, "The Spirit Dreams": Copyright
© 1969 by University of South Dakota. Chiron Khanshendel, "Grand-
father Pipestone Soul": Copyright © 1970 by Bronwen E. Rose. Duane
Niatum, "The Unfolding of Red Cedar Moon": reprinted by permis-
sion of Duane Niatum. Simon J. Ortiz, "War Poem": all rights reserved
by the author. Norman H. Russell, "anna wauneka comes to my ho-
gan": Copyright © 1970 by Midwest Quarterly. Sandy Robert Sando-
val, "Tight Mouth": Copyright © 1972 by Roberto Sandoval. Boots
Sireech, "My Son": used by permission of the author, former student
Institute of American Indian Arts. Eugene Tso, "I Am Hungry": from
Akwesasne Notes, Vol. 3, No. 3, April 1971. Turtle's Son, "Pyramid Lake

This book could not have been compiled
without the help of many people.
I want particularly to acknowledge my indebtedness
to Nan Braymer, A. Grove Day, Leah Lawentman,
Lillian Lowenfels, Clarence Major, Betita Martinez,
Lucille Medwick, Lois Michel, John Milton,
Michael Nichols, Rarihokwats, Jerome Rothenberg,
Madelyn Shulman, Stan Steiner
and Nan A. Talese.

Contents

Introduction   xxi

Indian Poems

Introduction: Some Notes on Indian Poems: SIMON J.
     ORTIZ/GLORIA TRUVIDO   3

ALTA: Thanksgiving   9

ACON, ROBERT: Mister Scoutmaster   10

BEACH, MARION "TUMBLEWEED": A Song to the Chicago Indian
     Village   11

BELL, JUANITA: Indian Children Speak   12

BIG EAGLE, DUANE: Bidato   13

BIRD, DOLLY: Return to the Home We Made   14

BLOCKCOLSKI, LEW (SHORT FEATHERS): Museum Exhibition
     18

BRIGHAM, BESMILR: North from Tanyana   19

BRUCHAC, JOSEPH: Indian Mountain   21

CARDIFF, GLADYS: Dragon Skate   23

COLFAX, GREG: *from* The River Never Named   25

CONCHA, CARL: The Spirit Dreams   26

CONLEY, ROBERT J.: We Wait   27

COYOTE 2: Alcatraz   29

EDMO, ED: I'm Not Going to Get Burnt Out   31

GOVAN, DONALD: Courage   32

HAIHAI PAWO PAWO: Alcatraz . . . Lives!!   33

JOHNSON, SANDRA: We Sprang from Salt Water   34

KENNY, MAURICE: Monahsetah . . . A Cheyenne Girl   35

KHANSHENDEL, CHIRON: Grandfather Pipestone Soul   36

LA FARGE, PETER: Autumn 1964   38

LEIVAS, JUNE: No Indians Here   39

LOPEZ, A.: Direction   43

MOMADAY, N. SCOTT: Earth and I Gave You Turquoise   44

NIATUM, DUANE: Ascending Red Cedar Moon   45

OLIVER, BETTY: The People Call for Justice   47

ONE STAR: Poem   48

ORTIZ, SIMON J.: War Poem   49

RANSOM, W. M.: Grandpa   51

RED CLOUD, FRED: White Man Says to Me   53

RUSSELL, NORMAN H.: anna wauneka comes
     to my hogan   54

ST. CLAIR, DARREL DANIEL: Only in Silence   55

PAULZINE, NIKI: Untitled   57

SAINTE-MARIE, BUFFY: *from* My Country, 'Tis of Thy People
     You're Dying   58

SANDOVAL, SANDY: Tight Mouth   59

SIREECH, BOOTS: My Son   60

SMITH, RICHARD: Till Forever and More   61

VIGIL, VICKIE: Native Tongue   62

TEESETESKIE, RAYMOND: My Kind of School   63

TEKAHIONWAKE: The Cattle Thief   64

TSO, EUGENE: I Am Hungry   66

TURTLE'S SON: Pyramid Lake 1970   68

VIZENOR, GERALD ROBERT: Haiku   69

WELCH, JAMES: Getting Things Straight   70

WHITECLOUD, TOM: Thief   71

YOUNG BEAR, RAY: Through Lifetime   72

Chicano Poems

Introduction: RICARDO SÁNCHEZ   77

ALURISTA: Mis ojos hinchados   80

ALVAREZ, JORGE: Autobiography in Maize   82

BELLAGENTE, MARINA DE: I am the land. I wait.   84

CÁRDENAS, RENÉ: La muerte del Sr. Durán   85

DELGADO, ABELARDO: Icon   87

D'ESPOSITO, ANTHONY: In Five Hundred Years   88

ESTUPINIAN: In Our House   89

LORES, MANUEL CHAVARRIA: Indian, You Travel   90

ARCIA, JUAN: My People   91

ARCIA, LUIS: The Cage   92

OMEZ, MANUEL: We Are Beautiful!   93

GONZALES, RODOLFO: *from* I Am Joaquin   94

GRAFFITTI: 7th Street   97

GUTIERREZ, JOSÉ ANGEL: 22 miles   98

HERRERA, JOHN FELIPE: A Certain Man   101

JAMES, DONNA: Cresciendo en el barrio   102

JÁUREGUI, M.: Untitled (sin titulo)   105

JUNGE, M.: Upon Submitting Proposals for Federally
    Funded Summer Programs   108

LOPEZ, DIANA: Sestina: Santa Prisca   110

LOPEZ, GABRIEL O.: Doing Time   112

MARTINEZ, RAMÓN: Cow Comes Home   113

MONTOYA, JOSÉ: Sunstruck While Chopping Cotton   114

ORTIZ, ORLANDO: Reflections of an Inarticulate Childhood
    116

SAAVEDRA, GUADALUPE DE: IF You Hear that a Thousand
    People Love You   118

SALINAS, OMAR: Aztec Angel   119

SÁNCHEZ, RICARDO: Introduction to Abelardo   121

STANCHI, HUGO: To Buss's Grandma   122

TALAMANTEZ, LUIS: *from* (Reflections) of a Convict   123

TIGRE: To Venture   127

VARGAS, ROBERT: Blame It on the Reds   128

Eskimo Poems

Introduction: MADELYN SHULMAN   135

ANGAIAK, JOHN: My Native Land, the Beautiful   138

NALUNGIAQ: Heaven and Hell   139

PICKERNALL, CLARENCE: This Is My Land   140

SAMIK: Hunger   142

TUKTU: Children of Nunamiut   143

IGJUGARJUK'S SONG   145

ANONYMOUS: Eskimo Songs   146

ANONYMOUS: Men's Impotence   154

ANONYMOUS: Who Comes?   155

ANONYMOUS: The Dead Hunter Speaks Through
the Voice of a Shaman   156

ANONYMOUS: The Song of Kuk-Ook, The Bad Boy   157

ANONYMOUS: Dead Man's Song Dreamed by One
Who Is Alive   158

ANONYMOUS: In What Shape?   159

ANONYMOUS: a woman's song about men   160

ANONYMOUS: the old man's song, about his wife   161

ANONYMOUS: spring fjord   162

ANONYMOUS: the choice   163

ANONYMOUS: dream   164

ANONYMOUS: Utahania's Impeachment   165

ANONYMOUS: spider   166

ANONYMOUS: Travel Song   167

ANONYMOUS: song of the old woman   168

Hawaiian Poems

Introduction: The Hawaiian Oral Tradition   171

Dirge   174

KIMURA, LARRY: For Ha'Alo'U   175

The Water of Kane   176

The Kumulipo   177

The Night-Digger   180

From a chant to Kualii   182

Lamentation for Lahainaluna   184

the woman who married a caterpillar   186

Taunt Song   187

Puerto Ricans in the U.S.A.

Introduction: DAVID HERNÁNDEZ   191

CARRERO, JAIME: Neo-Rican Jetliner   197

CRUZ, VICTOR HERNANDEZ: Afterword   206

FIGUEROA, JOSÉ-ANGEL: a conversation w/coca cola   208

HERNÁNDEZ, DAVID: Señora Medelez   212

LEDESMA, JESUS, JR.: Chicago Is a Hell of a Place   214

LLUBIEN, JOSÉ: City Poem V   215

LUCIANO, FELIPE: Spies going to the cooker   217

MARTINEZ, CARMEN: ugliness #5   219

MÁRZAN, JULIO ARCÁNGEL: An American Dream   220

PIETRI, PEDRO: Broken English Dream   221

THOMAS, PIRI: A First Night in El Sing Sing Prison   224

VILLEGAS, JUAN: WSLUM Presents   226

Related Poems by White and Black Americans

Introduction: CLARENCE MAJOR   231

ADNAN, ETEL: The Battle of Angels   233

BLY, ROBERT: Anarchists Fainting   234

BRAND, MILLEN: Behold Beloved   236

CABRAL, OLGA: General Custer Enters Hell   238

CARRUTH, HAYDEN: At Dawn   239

CHILDRESS, WILLIAM: For an Indian Woman
    Dead in Childbirth   240

CONNELLAN, LEO: This Is A Stick-Up   241

DAVIS, JEFFERSON: John Mason Gets Sassacus' Head   242

FLAHERTY, DOUGLAS: Snake Rite   244

GILL, JOHN: Something More Ghostly   245

HAINES, JOHN: The Traveler   247

HARMON, WILLIAM: Adaptation of Nahuatl Lament   248

HARPER, MICHAEL S.: Prayer: Mt. Hood and Environs   249

HOLMAN, J. C.: *from* Windsinger   250

INEZ, COLETTE: Los Quatros Ijadas De Una Palabra   251

KONOPACKY, ELIZABETH: Indian Tutoring Collage   252

LEE, AL: The Rage of Jackson   254

LEGLER, PHILIP: Campos Santo   256

LE SUEUR, MERIDEL: I Light Your Streets   257

LEVY, D. A.: the bells of the Cherokee ponies   258

Contents [xviii

LOURIE, DICK: the Indian on the moon   259

LOWENFELS, WALTER: At Bemidji Falls   260

MCCORD, HOWARD: A Day's Journey
with Geoffrey Young   261

MCGRATH, THOMAS: *from* Letter to an
Imaginary Friend   266

MAJOR, CLARENCE: Queen Pamunkey   269

MILTON, JOHN R.: El Turista en El Pueblo   270

MOORE, ROBERT NELSON, JR.: An Offering to the Dawn Princess
271

MOOS, MICHAEL: Cheyenne River Valley   273

NICHOLAS, MIKE: The Unbuilt Sand Castles
of Hawaii   274

OLSON, CHARLES: Maximus, to Gloucester, Letter 157   275

OVERTON, RONALD: Found Poems   277

OWEN, GUY: Who Speaks For The Red Man?   279

PIERCY, MARGE: Curse of the earth magician on a metal land
280

RAY, DAVID: The Indians Near Red Lake   282

RICH, ADRIENNE: 8/1/68   284

ROGERS, B. H.: *from* The Man Above the Land   285

RUMAKER, MICHAEL: Poem   286

SCHECHTER, RUTH LISA: Along Missouri   287

SMITH, RAY: A Fragment for Last Pony
of the Dacotah   288

STAFFORD, WILLIAM: People Who Went by in Winter   290

STEINER, STAN: But, the Africans Walked at Night   291

TAGGARD, GENEVIEVE: The Luau   294

TROUPE, QUINCY: Red Bone Pot Lunch   296

VERMONT, CHARLIE: Dream   297

VINZ, MARK: Dakota Death Song   298

WALSH, MARNIE: John Knew-The-Crow   299

WANTLING, WILLIAM: Initiation   300

WEEKS, RAMONA: An Aleutian Illusion   301

WHITE FEATHER, ANNA: Near Tassajara Bon Owl
—to be sung   303

WILLARD, NANCY: I can remember when there
were trees   304

WILSON, KEITH: Koyemsi   306

WOFFORD, PHILIP: The Old and the Young Dance
Separately   307

Traditional Indian Poems

Introduction: RARIHOKWATS   311

HHE-THA-A-HI: Eagle Wing: Dated 1881   313

ABENAKI: The Parted Lovers   314

APACHE: Songs of the Masked Dancers   315

CHEROKEE: To Destroy Life   318

DWAMISH: Chief Seattle Speaks   319

SOUTHERN CALIFORNIA: The Eagle's Song   320

CHIPPEWA: My Love Has Departed   321

HAVASUPAI: Sun, my relative   322

IROQUOIS: Death of a Son   323

MESCALERO APACHE: Dawn Song   325

NAVAJO: A Prayer of the Night Chant   326

NAVAJO: From a Sand Painting   327

NAVAJO: The War God's Horse Song   328

NEZ PERCÉ: Chief Joseph's Surrender Speech   330

NEZ PERCÉ: Smohalla Speaks   331

OJIBWAY: Song of a Man About to Die
in a Strange Land   332

PAIUTE: In the Beginning   333

PASSAMAQUODDY: Star Song   334

PLAINS CREE: Another Happening Was . . .   335

S. B. (WINNEBAGO): Peyote Vision   336

TEWA: Song of the Sky Loom   337

ZUNI PRAYER: That their arms may be broken
by the snow   338

ZUNI: Sun Rays   339
ZUNI: The Coming of My People   340
Lament of a Man For His Son: Son, my son!   341

Biographical Notes   343

Introduction

The natives of the American Empire have been living here for some twenty-five thousand years. I presume they will survive another twenty-five thousand.

Long after the white civilization has fulfilled its destiny—whatever that may be—our older brothers will be here. In what form no one can foretell. But you can be certain they will be singing and speaking poems as they have throughout their long history.

What we have in this book therefore is not only a collection of past poems but a foresight into poems to come.

Native Americans carry their past with them. They have what Anglos would call "long memories." Actually for them all time tends to be in the present.

"Time is really a circle (cycle)," Rarihokwats writes. "In some ways a fire also is symbolic of what this means—for within a fire are the ashes, the past, the flame and heat and light—the present. And there is also the wood yet to be consumed—the future. And yet the wood is something out of the past, and the ashes go back to the soil to be part of the future.

"The native peoples are made from this land, children of the Earth Mother. They are as old as the Rockies, as fresh as a cool spring, as mysterious as a sprouting seed. They walk about this land with the sure footsteps of a man in his own home, knowing they have been here before, belong here now, and will be here still when the cycles have spun a thousand turns."

We younger brothers whose past in this land is only a few hundred years are separated from the earth. Not only by cement roads and buildings but by our "short memories." We do not echo any earth or oral tradition. A few facts selected on behalf of the Great White Fathers are drilled into us at school. For us each few years history tends to start afresh. The Fourth of July has become a vacation. Our epics of Black, Red, Brown and labor resistance have to be learned outside the schools. Naturally our poems differ from those of the Earth People. Anglo poems grow out of a three-hundred-year past in this land. Even there, few of us echo our murders of the natives.

The struggle to be part of the earth goes on in many ways. In this book we do find Anglos who relate, just as we will find some in all the struggles that the Native and Black people carry on for their lives.

We are dealing here in these pages not with an art of words separate from other things people do. The poems of the Older Brothers, no matter how young they are, are a natural part of the way they live and communicate with each other and the world.

One young Puerto Rican poet says—if you want to change my poems go ahead, they belong to you. There is no "audience" in the formal sense, no space between the poem, the poet and anyone else, no stage on which there stands A Poet, and far away those who listen. Here the listeners are part of the poem. Darrel Daniel St. Clair, a Tlingit Indian born in Alaska, was in his teens when he wrote:

My school the earth.
My teachers,
The sky, the clouds, the sun, the moon.
The trees, the bushes, the grass,
The birds, the bears, the wolves,
The rivers, whom I claim to be
My mad genius.
Once I missed a day
Because they tried to make
Me learn it from the books
In a little room
That was really too stuffy.
I hope my teachers don't
Put me on the absent list.
I enjoy going to that school
Where the air is fresh.
Where nothing is said and I learn
From the sounds.
From the things I touch,
From all that I see.
Joy to the world and
I've fallen in love with my teachers . . .*

* From his book, *From the Wilderness to Bewilderness*, Magpie Press, Anchorage, 1970.

In our epoch a central problem for everyone is to survive, and we read poets to find out how they did it.

A poem serves to knit the edges of our language together, reveals for an instant, in the vitality of today's common speech, the possibility of becoming our whole selves. It should be talked about in a practical way—Claude Roy, the French critic, said—measuring its weight in happiness and profundity the way one measures the vitamins and calories in food.

"We live inside circles of ourselves." (Emerson) The essential framework around us is always in danger of escaping our grasp because it's in the next degree of vision. It's that degree which the poets in *From the Belly of the Shark* spell out for us.

If the earth could read this spelling it would have no difficulty in recognizing the poems in this book for its own. Not only because many of them relate to sky and air and sea and land; whatever the themes, the poems come from earth people. Perhaps that helps account for the predominantly youthful character of *From the Belly of the Shark*. It reflects the earth's ever-recurring spring which geologists estimate has several billion years ahead of it. The Eskimo poet's "This Is My Land" is typical of voices that will not be silenced on this continent as long as the grass shall grow. That applies not only to the Indians and Eskimos but also to the Chicano and Puerto Rican poets, whether they write of the land or of the barrio.

Consider for a moment the elementary problem of being alive in the United States. On one hand we are, as a people, as a country, infants—less than two hundred years old. On the other hand our civilization seems to be in a supersenile stage.

It's within that framework that *From the Belly of the Shark* offers a verbal relation to emotions that are perpetually young —love among people and the nature from which they arose, and anger at the conquistadores.

Today our best poems are short. We are not in an age that produces Homeric epics. But I suggest that this book as a whole does have an epic character. This is indicated in the title. As far as the white world goes, the one theme that dominates *From the Belly of the Shark* is: We want out!

"Really great poetry is always (like the Homeric or Biblical canticles)," Walt Whitman said, "the result of a national spirit and not the privilege of a polished and select few."

In what way do poems by Native Americans relate to the white poetry world?

The United Nations Convention on the Prevention and Punishment of the Crime of Genocide (adopted 1948) states that genocide includes "causing serious bodily or *mental* harm to any group."

The white poetry scene in the United States is in control of a literary syndicate. It is divided up into different families each of which has its favorite critics and anthologists, all of whom exclude nonwhite poets.

A recent example: *Alone With America: Essays on the Art of Poetry,* by Richard Howard (New York, 1969). It does not mention one nonwhite person. This "comprehensive study" of contemporary American poets has been widely reviewed and praised. Not a single critic mentioned the fact that its 594 pages should have been called *Alone With White America.*

A list of anthologies and books of criticism that exclude or deny the stature of poets of color takes several pages in *Books in Print.* I drew attention to this "white only" policy nineteen years ago in a review of a book which I said should be called *The Oxford Book of White American Verse.*

Aside from my own multiracial anthologies, only one or two anthologies contain a token Black poet, but even that is exceptional. Young Chicano and Indian poets are even more invisible to the white poetry junta. There are several Chicano poetry publishers; also over twenty-five Chicano newspapers and an outstanding magazine, *El Grito.* All publish poets who are completely eliminated by the white poetry rulers.

The New York Review of Books, The Saturday Review, The New Republic, The Nation and the other white publications (including most "little magazines") all participate in the White Poetry Syndicate.

What's at stake is not solely a literary affair; it is part of a genocidal attack on people of color. Those who deny the stature of Red, Black and Brown artists are accomplices in the murder of nonwhite people that continues throughout the United States, not only with police guns, but with job rejection, poverty and slums.

Speaking of Third World People, Aimé Cesaire has told us: "The people know that all creation, because it is creative, is participation in a combat for liberation . . . But cultural crea-

n, precisely because it is creation, disturbs. And the first
ng it disturbs is the colonial hierarchy because it converts
e colonized consumer into a creator . . . For the colonizer all
ligenous creation is unaccustomed and therefore, danger-
s . . .

"It is the task of the poets, the artists, the writers, the men
culture, by blending in the daily round of sufferings and
nials of justice . . . to create those great reserves of faith,
ose great storehouses of strength from which the people can
aw courage in critical moments, to assert themselves and to
sault their future."

What is it that keeps white critics away from the poetry of
ack, Brown and Red Americans? A key problem is its na-
onal or ethnic quality. Although their poems range through
any subjects, their work has a verbal texture that is unique.
ney draw not only from the world literary traditions to which
l poets are indebted, but also from their own oral traditions,
eir music, songs, special ways of speaking to each other. A
oung Indian said recently: "We don't have poets in my tribe,
d the people *talk* in poetry."

My approach isn't that we should "do something for non-
hite poets," rather, we should do something about the stand-
rds of poetry that white critics and readers have developed.
the field of poetry most white liberals have shark skins and
e proof of racism in their own field rolls off.

The genocidal rejection of poets of color has set up a
seudostandard of what constitutes poetry in the United
tates. It is part of an approach which also excludes many of
ne best new white poets whose work is already classic in the
oetry underground. White poets from Bukofski and Cabral to
chechter and Wantling, as well as nonwhite poets from At-
ins to Sánchez, Saavedra and Welch, are victims of a literary
anta whose rule extends throughout the schools and colleges
nd the white bookshops of the United States.

Black poets are now available in a number of Black an-
hologies and it is not proposed to duplicate those collections
ere. *From the Belly of the Shark* is unique in that it brings
ogether for the first time representative poems by descend-
ants of the original inhabitants of our country.

Poems, songs and stories by Indians have been published in
English since the days of Henry Rowe Schoolcraft (1793–1864).

One recent Whitman scholar, Maurice Mendelsohn, ma
tains that Whitman was influenced in developing his uniq
style by translations of Indian poems which were beginni
to appear as he started *Leaves of Grass*. Eskimo poems ha
also been available since Knud Rasmussen included some
the accounts of his polar expeditions. Chicano poems are
more recent development.

However, the Indian and Eskimo poems that were kno
were not considered part of the white "poetry tradition," a
were available only in specialized books. They were not i
cluded in anthologies, textbooks or studies and histories
"American literature."

Our selection is made up mostly of young contemporari
but some traditional Indian tribal poems are included. Thi
believe is in keeping with Indian tradition which is basical
a vocal tradition where all the past is present now.

Black, Brown and Native Americans are all nationaliti
within the United States, all part of our multiracial countr
They have their own way of speaking, their own music a
cultural patterns. The crime of the white literary junta is
deny this cultural validity to over thirty millions living in tl
United States. In doing so they deprive all white people of tl
vast emotional resources and insights that Indian, Black an
Chicano people express in their poetry.

In the United States whites are in danger of being d
stroyed as human beings by their inability to recognize tl
humanity and creativity of other ethnic groups. People
color aren't alone in America. They are part of the five-sixtl
of the earth that constitute the majority.

WALTER LOWENFEI

Indian
Poems

Introduction: Some Notes on Indian Poems

Two young Indian poets discuss their approach to the craft

SIMON J. ORTIZ [Pueblo]

Indian oral poetry is known to have existed as long as the Indians themselves. Some of it has been transcribed into English by various ethnologists, anthropologists and other students of Native American cultures, but written Indian poetry is something new.

The few Anglos who know any Indian poetry at all know the old tribal poetry through translation; they are not aware of recent developments. It is only in the past decade that some of us are beginning to write poems in English—not only Momaday, who is well-known for his Pulitzer Prize novel, but James Welch and others included in *From the Belly of the Shark*.

When I began to think seriously of being a poet, I looked for someone among my people who was writing poems. At that time I could not find anyone at all. Scott Momaday was still at the University of New Mexico as a graduate student; he hadn't had anything published. There was no one. There were some translations of oratory done by Chief Joseph, and autobiographical works done by anthropologists, but they did not present what I at least felt then was an art form. Of course, some of my views have changed on that.

About poems, it's not important to be analytical toward what you are saying and what you are listening to. What is important is that these words are coming into you and you are using these words. Not for the sake of recollection twenty or thirty years from now, or even to pass on to your children. If you are doing the right thing, it's just naturally going to be part of your children, of your future. It's not really important to note them carefully or definitely for the sake of being preserved to put into some musty old library. That may be why our people made no special effort in the past to record their songs and poems or do translations. They must have taken it for granted that it was better to have a living useful language rather than a written one to be stored away in memory banks.

I didn't think that the tribal poetry in which I had par-

ticipated was poetry until I began to notice the Japanese, C
nese and other Eastern philosophers. I began to read a little
Zen when I was eighteen or nineteen; and then I began
realize that I could also write, could also make notes of
activities around home, some of the songs, and write out of
context of these. I guess what would be ideal would be to rea
become a priest in the ceremonial fraternities.

There are about two hundred fifty languages spoken by Nat
Americans. I myself am a Pueblo Indian and my people
long to the Keresan linguistic stock. We don't all speak t
same language, although the people are the same througho
the nineteen Pueblo groups. Our language is, of course, e
tirely spoken. Most of our history was passed down to
through the myths transmitted from one generation to a
other. I don't understand the language of any other tribe
can just barely recognize when Navajo is being spoken. I
speak in my own language, I find I don't have to explain
much, because if you know the language, much of the histo
you would already know. And of course language does depen
on this. Whereas English pretends to be a very technical la
guage, Indian tongues don't seem to be as technical—they a
more of a spiritual language.

So far as my own poems go, sometimes I quite deliberate
put myself in an Indian frame of reference. Then I try to g
as near the meaning in English as possible. That is, I think th
poem in my own tongue, then redo it in English.

Last night I was in New York, and we were talking abo
the city, about how you can become stimulated and work crea
tively in the city. And I was asking myself why? I said tha
probably a person does creative work because he tries to real
identify or maintain himself as an individual within the cit
Against the pressures of that city form of life. Whereas in th
country he more or less follows the rhythm of the countrysid
He doesn't have all these hassles. He knows where he is a
Whereas, in the city, he doesn't, and by his struggles, by th
intensification of the pressures and by his response to them
his attempts to maintain himself as an individual—out of thi
come his creative products.

So far as realizing and maintaining a close relationshi

h nature, with Mother Earth, all Indian tribes are pretty
ch the same in our philosophical foundation, our ap-
aches. The songs are different but the myths I learned I
d are similar to those of other tribes.

In our native tongues we say poems to each other in the
ious ceremonies, the dances, the religious ceremonies,
ich are pretty much closed to the public. Of course, the
ems here are the songs and prayers. There are a few new
gs every year—but some of them remain traditional—the
itative poems are the prayers, some of them hundreds of
ars old.

Something like *From the Belly of the Shark* is very neces-
ry. There is some form of revolution going on today among
American people. Some part of it is taking place among the
icanos and the Indians—a lot of it is initiated by the Black
ople. And the Indian people have become very active re-
ntly. We must show that we are as valid as any other ethnic
racial group; our feelings must be recorded; our art in any
rm is very important.

I read *The White Syndicate* and I agree that what has
ppened was quite deliberate—my people and other ethnic
oups have been shunted aside for power purposes. Non-
cognition of our people adds to the power and the sense of
periority of the people in control. Even the history of our
ibes is denied to our young people when they go to school. My
vn group, the Ackumo Pueblo, participated in the history of
e Southwest, but the Indian students aren't taught anything
bout Ackumo culture or history.

We have become whitewashed. American history taught in
igh school and in grade school makes no mention of Indian
xistence. In many cases they don't even mention some of the
eaties. I think this is deliberate—in the sense that the army,
epresenting the United States government, had a policy of
xtermination against the American Indian. The pilgrims
aw our people here as naked savages with no sense of human
dignity—as defined in their terms. As an extension of this,
vhite people don't recognize what they took away from the
ndians in terms of land and self-respect.

Our poems, like our ceremonial dances and all our cultural
activities, do speak for us and they should not be denied.

GLORIA TRUVIDO [Pomo]

I am the real American, I am a Pomo Indian, I am a hum
being. Yes, I am the real American and that's why I am a bla
nigger Indian. I'll never forget the injustices done to me a:
child. My injustice was their glory and that is the only glc
they will ever know.

They teach in the history books that the Indian was the fi:
American, the only true American. Yes, I am the real Amer
can and that's why I am a black nigger Indian on this eart
in school, in the streets, in the show, in life. I am a black nigg
Indian and that's why they call my house a shack, my fath
a wino.

Being a real American black nigger Indian, I was poor; a
they laughed because sometimes I had to take pancakes
tortillas and beans for my lunch, they laughed, made sport c
tormented the poor little Indian girl and while they laughe
this black nigger Indian girl learned hate and bitterness, stoc
in tears and became strong. These things that happened to m
are not figments of my imagination, but real, real like I am
human being, real like I am poor, real like I dislike the ave:
age white American intensely, real like life. When I was si:
teen I entered an average American high school. My chile
hood tormentors had grown up and were now high schoc
students, only it was worse, because there were more. Ther
were other Indians, but they followed the white students, too
their ways, they turned their backs to me, were ashamed c
me. Ashamed because I was crude, ashamed because I wa
original, ashamed because I was a poor Indian, ashamed be
cause I was a disgrace to them. To them and the white stu
dents I was nothing and in my eyes they were average, dul
human beings. How strange it would feel to be an average
white American, so very dull.

It's ugly to be poor and yet it's beautiful, you learn to value
food even if it's a pound of cheap hamburger, fried potatoes
a fifteen-cent cupcake, and milk is always a splendor.

I am poor and my people are poor, poor so you people
can make yourselves look good. I am a black nigger Indian
and I am a dropout and why am I? I am a dropout because
of discrimination, because of white punks, because of white
girls who think they are top brass class, because I'm nobo-

's dog, because I'm nobody's slave, because I don't bow
down to anyone, because too many years my education has
insisted of hate and bitterness. I am a dropout because of
ignorance, a student in the Z class which is the lower
achievement class. I am no brain, but neither am I igno-
rant, school didn't do me any good, it made me look dumb
and I knew I wasn't. I have accomplished much for a low
IQ student, an ignorant black nigger Indian, and who
would have guessed it—certainly not all those bright stu-
dents in the X and Y classes or the white average Ameri-
can society. One would think a black nigger girl like me
would have shacked up with a number of guys and had
about two or three kids by now. One would think a black
nigger Indian girl like me would have been on the welfare
using the poor hard-working taxpayers' money.

Yes, one would think, especially the average American, a
black nigger Indian girl would have become a whore, a tramp,
nothing in life, a burden to the taxpayer. This is one Indian
that will not be a burden to the so-called great white race, and
they do think they are great. Pray to your Lord that I might
find forgiveness in my heart for those American Hypocritical
innocences. Go to your churches and pray and speak of broth-
erhood and come out into the world and make a hell for not
only a poor black nigger Indian girl but also a white trash
Okie; I am black and she is white, but our hell was the same.
The things that I do, the things that I write, the things that I
say are not just for a black nigger Indian, but for a white trash
Okie girl and she was American, they called her scum, she
was a human being and she cried and they were unaware and
they didn't care for they were perfect. They went to Sunday
School, they had a decent mother and father, they had knowl-
edge, they were white, they were nothing, an empty shell of a
human being. They shall live in their little boxes and be aver-
age and dull. How beautiful to be poor and eat tortillas and
beans, to eat acorn mush and a piece of flank. How beautiful
to be poor and be among a bunch of drunks and know their
sorrow, their anger, their hate, their bitterness, to know them
as people, as human beings and not as scum. How beautiful to
be poor and live in the bean field, to pick beans and be among
your people, to see the black, brown and white faces in the
fields mingled. When these people got mad they shouted their

anger, they were not hypocritical, they told each other the
hate and said, you White Trash Okies, damn Wetback Mex
cans, drunken feather-head Injuns, black Niggers, they spo
their hostilities and they were freed, they came together ar
they were the people.

I am a dropout because I wish to accomplish something
life, something of value to my people and other people.

My people are the welfare recipients, the winos who eat
the Mission, the people who toil in the fields, the braceros wl
people forget are human beings and tend to think of them a
automated machines.

My people are the poor and they are poor and they are ric

My people are the White Trash Okies who are my friend

My people are the Mexicans who are generous.

My people are the Negroes who took care of me when I wa
a child.

My people are the Pomo Indians and I am proud.

These are all my people, the only people I know and I am
glad I am part of these human beings, they are the people o
life.

Like the Pomo basket made from the roots of the earth I am
a strong descendant from the Indians and I will keep my herit
age as a Pomo Indian.

It is my essence to fight for equal human rights, so tha
someday my people will live on this earth as human being
and not scum of life.

It is far better to be a black nigger Indian that to be a foo
among fools, American Hypocritical Innocences.

Thanksgiving

So many dead Indians on the
kitchen floor
  can't open the oven to get
our 10-pound turkey.

The cranberry sauce is thick
and red.

Maybe next time it won't be
a brother's blood.

ROBERT BACON

Mister Scoutmaster

Aging Fred MacMurray God-and-country . . .
Where did you learn your woodland lore?
In the frontiers of East Orange, N.J.
Or in a box of cereal
Or from your grandmother
3/4 Cherokee, of course,
Who used to ride a horse
in a Wild East rodeo . . .
Oh, say can you see what you're doing to me?

Are you still scouting for Custer, Mister Scoutmaster?
You of the John Wayne brain
You with your Cub Scouts follow Akela—
Grown white men playing cowboys and Indians
(Without the cowboys).
So, you've seen the error of your ways, eh?
You now play only Indian
While Germans play Jews, I guess.

What will we do for the week's project?
The Eagle Scouts will dig Indian bones in Illinois.
While the last generation—
Kills eagles in Wyoming.

MARION "TUMBLEWEED" BEACH [Creek]

A Song to the Chicago Indian Village
[Wrigley Field, U.S.A.]

All is hushed at Flanders Field
All is desolate from the wrath of despair,
But no poppies wave here
Nothing lives here
Save two or three milkweeds sucking life blood
From a few rotting cross ties, and
Flies making a green market as they
Grub up the debris of this Fratricide.

Torn tents, bursted boxes, bursted cans
Lay strewn with bursted dreams.
A lonely Brave
With tear-filled eyes
With peach-fuzzed chin
Squats in the last standing tepee
Between bursted tom-tom and overturned bongo.

Nothing moves here
Save the greedy green flies
And the airconditioned cars of the Lighteyes.
Like vultures of the sky,
They circle, gawk, wonder and wait
For the fires of the funeral pyres;
But the Thunderbird, like the Phoenix,
Rises from the ashes of burnt mattresses, charred
        springs.
This is not Knee Bend . . . Kittanning.

Go tell it on the mountain
Over the hills and Everywhere
That the Indian still lives.

JUANITA BELL [Pima]

Indian Children Speak

People said, "Indian children are hard to teach.
Don't expect them to talk."
One day stubby little Boy said,
"Last night the moon went all the way with me,
When I went out to walk."
People said, "Indian children are very silent.
Their only words are no and yes."
But, ragged Pansy confided softly,
"My dress is old, but at night the moon is kind;
Then I wear a beautiful moon-colored dress."
People said, "Indian children are dumb.
They seldom make a reply."
Clearly I hear Delores answer,
"Yes, the sunset is so good, I think God is throwing
A bright shawl around the shoulders of the sky."
People said, "Indian children have no affection.
They just don't care for anyone."
Then I feel Ramon's hand and hear him whisper,
"A wild animal races in me since my mother sleeps
under the ground. Will it always run and run?"
People said, "Indian children are rude.
They don't seem very bright."
Then I remember Joe Henry's remark,
"The tree is hanging down her head because the sun
is staring at her. White people always stare.
They do not know it is not polite."
People said, "Indian children never take you in,
Outside their thoughts you'll always stand."
I have forgotten the idle words that People said,
But treasure the day when iron doors swung wide,
And I slipped into the heart of Indian Land.

DUANE BIG EAGLE

Bidato
[October Pomo Village]

Little Fawn gone to the river for water
First eyes light
Smoke hole sun circle
On the deer skin canvas
Breakfast haze warmed the rim of the valley.

Coyote came stealthily
From his camp in the North
Brown as the grass in the morning sun
Grey as the wood at the river run.

New Jerkins for Little Fawn
Drying on a rock
Apples buried deep in the hayed ground
Cold morning treat.

Sharing midday acorn mush
Coyote told of rain filled freshets
In bear country slopes.
Four hundred geese flew as he spoke
Snaking the air above the sullen river.

Drops hissed in the dust on the path
The ground drank
And winter rose
Blue-black from the ocean.

DOLLY BIRD

Return to the Home We Made

Hey my man
you know we can't
stay in these city trappings
You know it my man
so hey
we been squatting too long
on land that ain't never
gonna be ours

There's no jobs
and the want ads
offer equal opportunities
done filled this morning
Hey we're good
don't need this crud

From where we're at
we can see
a travel agency and
I don't guess I'm
for Miami this season
but oh hey let us
go Rocky Mountain delving

Remember where we used to live
when John Wayne never came around
and Gunsmoke came out
of your rifle
let's hock next year
for this instant
and when we sell out
next January

at least we will have spent
some good times

We have been null and void
a sight too long
I'm thinking we could
go home

And if we don't make it
we'd a done something

I've seen you remember
'cause I've seen you cry
Crying with dry eyes
and your blood bursting
at the thought
of untrod plains,
the beaver woods
and I've seen your eyes travel south
over the memorized outlines
of sun silhouetted buttes
down into a wash
before the August rains
when we spoke
a beautiful language
and the Gods watched us
We could see them too
as we huddled in a cave
of a canyon in a desert storm
when thunder rolled and
crashed against red orange
purple echo walls
and then a rainbow grew
where lightning was planted
Yes I know you cried
'cause I was crying too

I know you're aching
to ride the appaloosa
who knew your destination
by the mood of your kick
I did love to see
you all over leather
in the distance
and to feel
the trembling ground
as you rode closer
and nights with
a separate dusk and evening
when after fry bread
and fresh venison
we leaned our shoulders
into the rising heat
of our sacred fire

Oh strong man
please, we can't go on
remembering only
the home we made
out of what we found
and a warm quilts sleep
We must go back
We're talking sounds
that we don't understand
We're down but please
We could try

They've mock laughed at us
We awkward tripping from
the street to where people walk
the skin-burst clay
Our confused eyes
unable to focus

on all them at once moving
Your years molded muscles
are outmoded here
City people putting us down
as ignorant because
our knowledge is wisdom
not a library
and we ain't needed
here

Now, it must be now
our round trip
Complete the circle
while we can see
a flateared cougar
and can you tell
how many days passed
after these tracks of wolves
and which way is
the big snow blowing
and which is the root
to calm the fever

Now you lift your heart
with something stirring
starting to rustle in you
Asking me if we've
got enough salt 'n lard
and is dog sleeping
outside the door
and maybe we could
somehow get
a few sheep of our own
or cattle seeing as now
they're no trouble at all

LEW [SHORT FEATHERS] BLOCKCOLSKI

Museum Exhibition

In the mid-winter of frozen cattle,
sleeping sheep and hand-mown grain;
with our words dead and our blood spread,
we squat in peeling outhouses
of yesterday's movement.

Watching berry beads crack, deer leather
go black, and an old shield become
artifact, we search for exit signs
to the sun. Down ceramic hallways
lined with polished fishhooks,
prayer sticks and our gods' stories
the morning is a blurry slur.

BESMILR BRIGHAM [Choctaw]

North from Tanyana

these are the woman mountains

the without shame cold

the sun has circled around her breasts
and heated her pelvis
she sprawls
face up, stomach heaved full and loaded
the legs braced
thighs and knees holding in their long wait, belly
flat
    a child's game of statue whirled
in light, another
thrown under the pelvis
an arm from the chest is falling down
the upper arm held above, into
the clean spaces of air
lifts a breast softly

waiting for what giant who will take her

low trees brush up the sides of her legs
spread unprotected
the winds and the great thaws to ravish her
caribou bite at her nipples
wolves rove down from the thick edges of gravity
stand, in the defenseless waste
singular range
shapes on the high moors of silence
chains of silver snow against the throat

the woman—abandon mountains

the frame pierced cold
their buttocks and faces are turned sidewards as in
sleep
an avalanche of women
hurled from the peaks of winter, they lift toward the
          long awaited
from still valleys, lovers
the turf shines like green silk
over the young flesh of their shoulders

men riding down on golden horses
out of the snow

the sun has taken over all the pastures

young moose hide in the willow clumps
the sun is grazing on the open hills
the thick grass is fresh laid-out in patches
moves as light is moved
like a slaughter of hides
stretched clean for the tanning, as though
some certainty of hand had placed them

JOSEPH BRUCHAC

Indian Mountain

My father and I
walk up the mountain
follow the overgrown
logging road
saplings
maple and fire cherry
birch, alder,
willow and beech
catch at our feet
we carry
our deer rifles gently
knowing we cannot shoot them
we are climbing the mountain
white men named Big Pisgah

I stand beside
the beaver pond
in the notch between two peaks
my father gone before me
his late found love a memory
Canada geese land
gabbling in the distance
they sound
like a far off pack of hounds
My feet crush into
a fallen tree
its rotten hulk floats
in the night
alive with foxfire
I am climbing the mountain
white men named Little Pisgah

my hand held before me
like a lantern

Jacking deer
with a light back in '34
my Indian grandfather cruises
the old mountain road
in a battered Ford
fueled with hunger
his kids ate well that winter
jays scrapped for the suet
he hung from the trees
and you could choose
which would it be
starving in the snow's
grey cloud
or in sudden thunder
out of night
astonished by
the golden eye of a god

There is a stream which rises
from a place
half down the mountain
my father showed it to me
as he found it in a dream
the ghost of an old Indian
leading him
a wisp of fog
to its banks

I shall go to that last water
when I am old
when my blood runs
like the sad Hudson
heavy and damned

with the waste
I shall go there
and wade into that water
where the bottom is spread
with stones
that lie like bones of ancient
and beautiful animals
I shall spread my arms
in the sweet water
and go like a last wash of snow
down to Loon Meadow
in the last days of spring.

GLADYS CARDIFF [Cherokee]

Dragon Skate

What sound awoke me?
The grate of shells?
But I am not in the sea.
Who is there?
Do you know me?
One who knew me is dead.
The hag that took me from the beach is dead.
She took me,
Yanked my head back, and
My pectorals like broken wings, and
The plate of my body, and
My whip,
All of me distorted
In an S for sorcery.
I curled to a wizened dragon, brown as a scab,
On her drying rack.

Is this daylight foaming, ah flooding, my eye holes

Red, red?
I'm tight as a gut string.

Before her,
I moved, easy
Over the ocean's crust,
Undulating,
Mesozoic,
Swilling on mollusks,
Loving the sea bottom, myself
An ovoid kiss.
She
Kissed the backside of Satan.
Did her bones jig
Under the howling strappado,
Or does she,
Does she lie flat?
She buried me alive, the witch,
Trying to hide herself inside boxes, in dark corners,
Under the boards of her house,
In ashes.
And I, in agony
While the years gathered like silt in the cave of my
        face,
Waited,
Changed in this scorched bandage of a body.

Yet?
Are you there?
I arose from black fire.
I could move again.
Let me show you.
Why do you wait?
Lift me! Lift me!

GREG COLFAX

from The River Never Named

He is the riderless horse in the field
        of his mother's soul.

He is the abandoned eye of the never named rider.
        He faces the river

the light from the sky with no moon.
        The woman of all names

visits him in the growing silence of echoes.
        Always at the moon's river

in the desert's dry field, he drinks the voice
        of the never named,

swallows knowledge on his hands and eyes,
        stares at the vision in his palms,

raises his arms to the sky of all moons.

He is called Crazy Words of the Lake's fountain.
        I read in his genesis,

as a warrior's ceremony the diving into the never
        named, embracing the stone

        tracing the spirit's feather
        the soul shed's outline.

CARL CONCHA

The Spirit Dreams

Don't you know that you're not supposed to make love to mockingbirds?

Damn, how many times do I have to remind you that, if Rainbow Girl smears herself on the wall just one time, you must burn bones, not beans. Because then, the moon will glow at you, and maybe Mr. Skeleton will put on a dance for you in his closet. He'll stomp, rattle his bones, jingle his empty cells to the beat of your heart.

Watch it there, boy! The echoes of his chants might lead you wandering alone down that lonely road and, all of a sudden, spirits will come from all sides at you. They'll paint you in shocking pinks and hard-hitting blues.

Then they'll sew you into a water drum and, while you're floundering around in that half-filled drum, they'll beat the hell out of it.

Then you will see that it's not merely a birthday you're celebrating. By damn, you'll be forever tuned in and vibrating.

ROBERT J. CONLEY [Cherokee]

We Wait

1. White Blight

Crookneck Whiteblight, anthropologist,
Bermuda shorts & tennis shoes,
spectacles on nose,
in radiant pomposity rares back
in his chair, feet on desk.
Of course, the songs themselves have small
value for the serious scholar, though I, myself,
should probably acknowledge a certain indebt-
edness to the savage for filling out my biblio. But
the real thrill is getting the stuff they think in
their childlike simplicity is sacred. The success-
ful anthro. must be not only well-informed but
clever. And in the *cleverness*—ah, therein lies
the thrill. For instance, it's amazing what the
waving of a dollar bill can do; spirituality goes
up in smoke, so to speak, and you've got yourself
an article. I've had not a few successes with the
Amerinds.

2. The Earth

the earth is my mother
the grass is her hair
with your plows you are ripping her breast
I will not use a plow
nor will I cut the grass
nor herd and pen up my little brothers
the various animals
I cannot stop you
but I will not follow you.

3. [to be sung to the tune of
"A Mighty Fortress is Our God"]

Is it not wonderful to think
What God has done for man?
He's sent the white to save the red,
To take him by the hand,
To take his hand and lift him up
From darkness and from Sin,
To teach him how to work and pray,
Speak English and drink gin,
To cut his hair a decent way,
Wear pants and shirts and shoes,
To eat his food with knife and fork
And gracefully to lose.

4. USA

the cities are overcrowded
with people who are going crazy
streams are polluted
a man cannot swim in them
nor drink from them
neither can he eat with safety
the fish that swim in them
the air is not fit to breathe
there is violence on campus
violence in the streets
the crime rate soars and
a senseless immoral war drags on
the government is corrupt
and does not even know it
and the English language is degenerating
on all fronts into Madison Avenue drivel
we have maybe 30 yrs. (they say)

5. the old prophecy

ame in various forms
m the Creek
he Navajo
the message is always clear
ite men will come
ey did)
y will take the land
ey did)
y will nearly destroy the People
ey tried)
y will waste the land
ey have)
en they will go away
e wait).

OYOTE 2

catraz

epartmentalized interior decorations by Hickel
nokey the bearing of ill will promises
maximal Indianness upon the island rock,
ith the end of trail statues fashioned in metal
        monstrosities,
        Alcatraz, whose singing now is tribal youth,
        whose message to an insane world is courage,
        whose blood is the ancestor life stream
        surging and singing the ocean's tidal pull,
iplicated tribulations computerized into
conformities
our brother's keeper's Bureau of Indian
Annihilation,
here federal parks administer chain-reaction
madness

and paper pelicans nest the brink of treaties,
>Alcatraz, whose voice is born of dawn,
>whose dancing is of unity born of pain,
>whose echoes must resound in many hearts
>which have felt the iron heel of mad
>oppression,
political pollutions assembly-lined in the Madison
Avenue
of Nixonian nerve-gassed American atrocities,
four score and seven million military massacres ag
where pilgrims and pledges cannibalized a continer
>Alcatraz, whose children sprang from
>poverty,
>whose daily bread was prejudice and hate,
>whose very life depended upon white welfa
>in anger now, a kinship of Indian heredity,
Bankamericatharsis in cataclysmic lily-white
liberalizations
that all men are created equally endowed of genetic
genocides
that white is right and might is the
manic-manifestation
of paranoid patriotism excluding all of darker hue,
>Alcatraz, whose singing now is tribal youth,
>whose message to an insane world is courag
>whose blood is the ancestor life stream
>surging and singing the ocean's
>tidal pull . . .

ED EDMO

I'm Not Going to Get Burnt Out

I'm not
   going to get burnt out
with your amphetamines
      even though
my People's lodges
      were burnt
         by
      U.S. Cavalry
         and
"well-meaning" citizens

I will not
   be flooded out
      by YOUR
         cheap
            wine
               stale
                  beer
and strong whiskey
   even though
         backwaters
         of dams
cover our once sacred
            and
      promised grounds

I will not
      be
            pacified
by blue eyes

and
    blond hair
even though
      YOUR
"heroic" mountain men
    raped
     my
  great-grandmother

DONALD GOVAN

Courage

I saw Crazy Horse's
great vision
counting coup
down Franklin Ave.

drunk;

smiling at people
and
joking with children.

Down that ugly street
he staggered.

A death chant under his
breath
prepared for resurrection

beside great spirits
and a brave warrior's
rage.

HAIHAI PAWO PAWO

Alcatraz . . . Lives!!

You say they're gone????

       -All taken off . . .
       all pushed off . . .
       all pulled off . . .
       all ripped off . . .

You say they're gone????

Listen then, listen long—

       Hear that laughter . . .
       Hear that cry . . .
       Hear that child . . .
       Hear that prayer . . .

Listen then, listen long.

The winds carry their songs
The sun carries their warmth,
The winds carry their songs
The grass whispers their words.

You say they're gone????

       Listen, whiteman . . .
         Listen long . . .

SANDRA JOHNSON [Makah]

We Sprang from Salt Water

We sprang from salt water
  A meeting of waves.
Our men hollowed
  canoes
from logs
  with the bone of whale
and together rose
  as one
but were many
giving thanks to the sea.
With a song
      we were born
  startling the birds
      into flight
while the seagulls
      cried
  circling the air
      and following
the strain of our paddles
      moving us
  toward land.

Now our men
  keep returning to the sea
filled with the rhythm
      of salmon
fishing a strange beauty

through dark waters
as silver fins
    leap wildly over death
seeking the savage moment
    that saves
the young.
    Our people will not die.

MAURICE KENNY

Monahsetah . . . A Cheyenne Girl
(for the Hochs of Denver)

Evicted into the frozen teeth of winter
By the landlords of the Plains;
Cast into the bloody waters of the Washita
Where your father's corpse flowed in the stream . . .
His manhood stuffed into his mouth,
His scalp made guidon for Custer's soldiers.
Torn from the band of the helpless captive women,
Your suckling child, mewing and puking in your arms;

Driven by Long Hair to feel out the ashes of the villages,

Scout out the vital hearts of your people.

Did Sheridan's red hands fondle the sweetness
Of your young Cheyenne nipples;
Did Custer mount you like a stud until
His civil wife pulled his sweaty thighs
From off the Cheyenne mystery of your life!
You held your childish hands to your womb
And felt the kicking of a bird, the fledgling sperm
Planted like so much corn by yellow-locked Long Hair!

Where did you find the love to mount his cot,
        knifeless,
Or did he find your flesh upon his earthen floor!

Custer strutted your grave to glory, foolish girl!
Now in the winds of the Washita Valley cottonwoods
    cry
For the slain Cheyenne. No wind moans in the leaves
For the head-strong girl, daughter of Little Rock,
Who followed the tails of the pony soldiers.

CHIRON KHANSHENDEL

Grandfather Pipestone Soul

Grandfather pipestone soul
upon empty gambles,
upon rock-faced ones their eyes
just steel, boiled
noble savage. . . . hah hah
hah   Grandfather forgive them
you just weren't human
to their eyes, just a dirty
redskin in a golden city
really just adobe.
Grandfather your songs
like rain not gentle
necessary, hard sometimes
life—necessary.
Grandfather your dances
shut-eyed, stopped over, inward-bound
slowed but not stopped
just because your body died.
Grandfather I love you.
You didn't know me—unborn—

the embryo pipestone soul
(my chicken's-feet must have danced
my lips chanted
within mother then)
I hope you heard.

       DO YOU KNOW WHAT THEY'VE DONE?
What they have done to your family.
The ancestors would not like my name—
it's christians that gave it to me.
We're in California now.
Grandfather, they even moved us.
Some stayed that had the knowledge, but my kiva is
   closed,
my skin paled by eternal wet winter and
so—even my name is gone.
Grandfather I have never seen you
but someone inside-me knows your face.
Inside me you still dance,
inside me you still sing—
my heart is your drum, your grand-daughter's body
your rattle. I hope   when this body dies
someone remembers to make a paho for me
though I have no name and silence condemns me.
How many kivas are dead now, Grandfather,
and how many Grandfathers receive prayers where you
   are?

I send this to you while home is a museum
and our loved ones zoo specimens—and KNOW
that I love you and hear you still!

                December 4, 1970
                Kensington, California

PETER LA FARGE

Autumn 1964

Sitting here in the night with
darkness heaped in every corner,
wondering if you can read my writing,
because that's the only light I have.
The morning's coming. I can hear the
garbage trucks singing like city
crickets, collecting the night.
Thinking that of the new songwriters,
I'm the oldest and the most evil with
my past. I have no lies to tell
about my past and sometimes it
strangles me like a black dog putting
his foot down my throat. I am not so
wild as I was once; I'm pretty good
about it. I haven't gotten the rabies
of shadow in my teeth except once or
twice in the last six months. I
always rage most at those I love,
and mostly for good reasons. And to
those to whom I did, my apologies.
But you may have deserved it.

Someone once said to me "I envy
you your heart, but I couldn't stand
your hangovers." And oh, how I have
fallen for you, you high-stepping,
wrap-around chrome-popsicle girls.
For the right pair of legs, and God save us from
the probable barbed wire of blonde hair. And
I'll do it well, and if there are few men that

do that any more they get oriented to be sane
too soon. And it's because I am mad and can't
help it.

I always love like a high jack-rabbit going
through a bramble. Or a hawk up there twining the
world around him just before he falls to get the
jack, like an eight-wheeler going through a Kansas
town at midnight, with only a little boy watching
from his bedroom window and riding every non-stop
car out. I love like an act of nature.
Not casual, my love.
But like a tender trumpet.
Softly.
Proudly.
Loudly.
Lostly.
In the thunderheads my dark,
My love.
Not casual . . .

JUNE LEIVAS

No Indians Here

so you've gone sightseeing
on the reservation
your precious camera
hangs from your neck
and the angry noon day sun
releases the sweat
from the forehead you've mopped
a million times
with your monogrammed handkerchief
in stuffy executive meetings

you thought you'd get away from it all
and see the indians
living the easy life
but you're faced by those
unwilling to pose
in their hunger
hopelessness
and grief
these are the weary and the numb
the helpless and the dumb—
there ain't no indians there
they're just distrusting souls
who turn their backs
on the exploitation
of the camera's click
so take your camera back
to your executive meeting room
and snap a picture
of their destiny
in the making

you walk into the tribal council chambers
and stand on the plush carpets
surrounded by the reservation leaders
dressed in suits and wearing ties
so eager to tell you of the projects
that will help reduce
reservation unemployment
they show you the plans of the plants
that will bring the reservation up
to the standards you've set
the smoke-producing progress
that we fear in the cities
will take their toll in time
and all in the name of progress—
there ain't no indians there

they're just puppets
dangling on the dreams
of success and progress
you've tied them to

the indian culture center
on the college campus
guides you to the source and topic
of your term paper
and brings you to the indian student
who knows first hand
what it's all about
long-haired behind the desk
wearing beads and moccasins
talking of the good life that was
before you came
and how he plans to return to it
he is the traditionalist
before alcatraz posters
and indian leaders
geronimo's eyes
tell you no lies
and you think that this
is truly what you've been looking for—
that ain't no indian sitting there
he's just a dreamer
determined in his pursuit
of something to believe in
believing that yesterday
will return for him

you come into my house
where angela davis on the wall
stares back at you
and the posters cry out
revolutionary slogans

that hit harder than my words
and viva la raza tells you
that my blood is mixed
i'm sitting cross-legged
on the floor
with a book of malcolm x
open in my hands
your indianism tells you
there ain't no indian in this house
where there ain't no indian posters
and i'm seeing you through
little square glasses
and my eyes reflect your thoughts
there ain't no indians here
there is only me
but if you'd leave your alienation
nationalism
and racism
behind
i'll lead you by the hand
to the hills
the unmarked graveyards of time
beyond the pages of a history book
outside the glass cases of the past
and after you've seen it all
try if you can
to look into my eyes
and tell me that
there ain't no indians here . . .

A. LOPEZ [Papego]

Direction

I was directed by my grandfather.

To the East;
    So that I might have the courage
        of the bear.

To the South;
    So that I might have the wisdom
        of the owl.

To the North;
    So that I might have the craftiness
        of the fox.

To the earth;
    So that I might receive her fruit.

To the sky;
    So that I might live a life
        of innocence.

N. SCOTT MOMADAY [Kiowa]

Earth and I Gave You Turquoise

Earth and I gave you turquoise
   when you walked singing
We lived laughing in my house
   and told old stories
You grew ill when the owl cried
We will meet on Black Mountain

I will bring corn for planting
   and we will make fire
Children will come to your breast
   You will heal my heart
I speak your name many times
The wild cane remembers you

My young brother's house is filled
   I go there to sing
We have not spoken of you
I will follow her white way

Tonight they dance near Chinle
   by the seven elms
There your loom whispered beauty
   They will eat mutton
and drink coffee till morning
You and I will not be there

I saw a crow by Red Rock
   standing on one leg
It was the black of your hair
   The years are heavy
I will ride the swiftest horse
You will hear the drumming hooves

DUANE NIATUM [Klallam]

Ascending Red Cedar Moon
(for Philip and Ann McCracken)

I

Out of friendship and a slow retreat of the blood,
I step like coyote through petroglyphs
of spear, trap, and drum.
Streaming ocher threads over the salmon ceremony,
the rain falls in four directions.
Wind's chant walks like Grandfather around
the village, greeting the moss, shells,
berry and water baskets.
Children circle the Elders in half the moon
who are carving their lives on this totemic dream.

My son has run off somewhere,
perhaps to discover the thundering hawk,
the dark beauty of deer turning
to face him, vanish like sunlight down the path.
Or maybe he is learning how to fall,
make room for pain and the nightmare in his heart,
rest like a bear in the dark?
Like Niatum, his great-grandfather,
he believes the humor of bluejay,
the legends in a dive of the whale,
will lead him to fern-shadowed meadows,
the Elwha river's thousand-year elegy to Spring.
With the gift of the blind,
he may turn these roots into song or to dance.

My sweet woman, keeper of the poem,
floats like a waterbug,

a naked fan of sunlight.
I will lie with her soon in the soft,
secret room of willows.

2

In the owl's light, we darken with the fire
and the moon spreading its feathers
over the Ho-Had-Hun sky.
Now dancing in honor of the missing fathers,
the drums grow quiet as the river birds,
and we see the statlth step
from the memaloose illahees, the forest.
The Elders rise first in greeting;
it has been so long since the Klallams
have heard such weeping:
        "Chee chako. An-na-du! An-na-du!
        Mox-pooh.   Mox-pooh."

---

statlth: ghosts
memaloose illahees: graves
Chee chako: newcomers

An-na-du!: come!
Mox-pooh: lie still and then
        explode

BETTY OLIVER

The People Call for Justice

The People call for justice
White brother, do you hear?
Do the ghosts of the past
Walk at your side,
And does the bitterness of today
Close your heart to truth?
Kinzua
Drowning the history of the Seneca.
The mountain of the Pipestone
Now a place for unseeing tourists to gawk.
Where are the wampums of the Iroquois?
Locked in sterile glass
For sterile minds to view
While the home of the Delawares
Waits to disappear under the waters of Tocks
Where will our kindness stop?
When the last quiet man
Walks into Eternity?

ONE STAR

Poem

The native walks
The rural past
The urban paths
And the roads between
To test the dangerous drives
That play and pulse
Like roller coaster drops
And titawhirl spins
Careening around the zip-zoom moods
On former farm and country lanes
Recording and mapping.
Hoping
For a 4-leaf cloverleaf intercession
Hurtling him
Straight
Where
Someday
He may grasp control
At the steering wheel
And softly twist
A precise mixture of emotions
For the tender fuel system
of his soul

SIMON J. ORTIZ [Acoma Pueblo]

War Poem
[Oct. 15, Moratorium Day]

Santo Domingo, DemRep, March 1965.
I took part, attached
to the 82nd Airborne,
in the U.S. action to "save
the world for democracy."
We landed 35,000 troops
and turned part of Santo Domingo
into rubble and whores.

Acomita, Spring of 1966,
near my home, a couple nights before
the El Paso Natural Gas Co. line blew up.
The flames towered hundreds of feet upward.
Eulogio Garcia was saying, "I cried.
I got scared. It all came back to me.
I went in my bed when I heard it.
I was there. They told me
I was doing something for my people.
I am telling my children
that it is no good, that it does something
to a man's dignity."
Mr. Garcia, a WW I veteran.

George, a Mexican kid,
wrote me from Vietnam, 1967:
"You know, I feel bad,
this morning I dragged
a boy, V.C., I guess, from a hole.
He was hiding, & he was crying.

The sargent some punk kid
from Texas kicked him.
I was crying. He looking
like my little brother.
I'm part Indian myself, you know."

Yazzie, young Navajo Vietnam veteran
in Manhattan Bar, 1968, in Gallup.
"I don't know. I don't know."
We watched Nixon on T.V. declare
antiballistics in Montana.
Yazzie's hair still matted with blood.
Got clobbered by the cops.
Just got out of jail. "I don't know."
Shaking his head,
crying onto his Purple Heart.

Acomita, 1968, just off U.S. 66
in the village cemetery.
"He looked so goddam small,
maybe they cut something out of him,
cut him short," said Johnny Poncho
about Jerry Chino's military burial.

Rough Rock, 1969. This morning
I looked out at the flag.
Red and white and blue,
foreign matter whipping in the wind.
The sky is beautiful beyond it.
I think of mountains.
I think of the people.
I think of the harmony possible.

W. M. RANSOM [Northern Cheyenne]

Grandpa

Grandpa he was a man
he taught me the things that
          mattered
how to eat oxtail soup before
fishing on Saturday morning to
keep you warm how to
cast a line into a
streamful of angered anglers and
be the only one to
come home with anything worth
bragging about how to
set teeth in any saw and
dovetail a joint in a
chair leg and roof a
house and weld a
straight seam on a
kitchen pipe and make a
home out of a
workshop out of a
two-car garage and
smoke Granger's tobacco and
love work and kids and
fishing for "a Man's
life is his work and
his work is his life" and
once you take away his work
you pull the plug of his life
and it takes too long
for it to drain silently away.
One day they came and

told him to go home and
rest old man it's time
that you retire he begged
them "let me stay" but
they of course knew best for
everyone knows at sixty-five
all men are old and useless and
must be cast off to
rot so he came home and
tried to fish and
couldn't and tried to joke and
couldn't and tried to live and
couldn't. Every morning he was
up at four and cooked breakfast
      for
grandma and warmed up the house
      and
went to the workshop and
filed saws for neighbors but
they told him to stop that too
so he put all his tools away and
cleaned up the workshop and
came into the house for his
daily afternoon nap and
died. They didn't know
what I knew because he
didn't tell them but
he showed them
Grandpa he was a man.

FRED RED CLOUD

White Man Says to Me

save.
I save. String. Bricks. Trees.
Horses. Leather. Nobody wants
what I save. So I go into the
desert, rolling my ball of string
which is four feet in diameter.
Two white men come. They look at
the Bricks. Trees. Horses.
Leather. String. Where'd you
steal them things they ask.
they don't listen. they take
the string from me and they
twist it into rope. Now they
put the rope around my neck.
They hang me from one of the
trees I saved.

NORMAN H. RUSSELL [Cherokee]

anna wauneka comes to my hogan

anna wauneka comes to my hogan
she tells me
mother must go back to the hospital
who has the whiteman's disease
i say to anna we must ask my mother
my mother says no
I say to anna then she will not go
anna says that then she will die

then I tell anna wauneka that i think
my mother will die anyway
in the white man's hospital
that it is better for her to die here
than in that other house of the dead

when my mother dies
we will close the hogan
we will build another hogan
we will sing a song to my mother

this will not be for a long time yet
until that time comes
I will dress my old mother each morning
I will carry her into the new sunshine
so that she will see the dawn come
so that she will hear the bird sing.

DARREL DANIEL ST. CLAIR [Tlingit]

Only in Silence

O Alaskan Rain
When you begin to pour,
Remember these thoughts
Before you touch the earth,
That after you come,
Soak in to the minds of men
Yesterday's lost bits of love.

O Alaskan Wind
You are blowing very hard.
Pause a moment
Before you move on,
And after you are gone,
Take with you, Mother Purity,
And introduce her
to Man's inner soul.

O Alaskan Moon,
You have done your job well,
You are the night light
That creates night time beauty
And before you go down
Just remember,
that I, like others,
Am looking forward
To seeing you again.

O Great Alaskan Northern Lights,
You being the mystery of mysteries,
I tell you now,
To remain as such,
For already,

Man
is getting to know too much
For his own damned good.

O Alaskan Snow,
You come to my earth
By the millions
And you feel rather cold,
But let it be known
To the millions of my kind
That at least
You came in peace,
And left
in peace.

O Alaskan Sun,
You have shown me
What is warmth and light,
You have shown me
Your beauty which reflects
Off
The clouds, mountain tops and water,
And today,
Before you go down
To shine in another town
Remember to remind
The bodies of men,
That you
Are still the
Vitalness
To all growth.

O Alaskan stars,
You are the number
Of many unknown suns
Seen by us

Only at night,
You in the sky
Have created the "Big Dipper"
And gave the Alaskan man his pride
Which now stands proudly
As a design on the Alaskan flag.

O Great Alaskan Natives,
You have understood
These forces in silence
And have lived accordingly,
I know
It is hard to understand
What is happening today,
So this is my prayer
For all of us,
Amen.

NIKI PAULZINE

Untitled

i am the fire of time.
the endless pillar
that has withstood death.
the support of an invincible nation.
i am the stars that have guided
lost men.
i am the mother of ten thousand
dying children.
i am the fire of time.
i am an indian woman!

BUFFY SAINTE-MARIE

from My Country, 'Tis Of Thy People You're Dying

Hear how the bargain was made for
    the west
With her shivering children, in
    zero degrees
"Blankets for your land" so the
    treaties attest;
Now blankets for land is a bar-
    gain indeed—
But the blankets were those
    Uncle Sam had collected
From small pus-diseased dying
    soldiers that day,
And the tribes were wiped out
    and the history books
    censored!
100 years of your statesmen have
    felt it's better this way;
Yet a few of the conquered have
    somehow survived
Their blood runs the redder
    though genes have been paled;
From the Grand Canyon's caverns
    to Craven's sad hills
The wounded, the losers, the
    robbed sing their tale;
From Los Angeles County to up-
    state New York
The white nation fattens while
    others grow lean.

Oh, the tricked and evicted,
    they know what I mean:
My country, 'tis of thy people
    you're dying!

SANDY SANDOVAL

Tight Mouth

Indian with tight mouth
hard to understand except
if you live in Tohatchi
the wind dries and robs

water with every
word spoken precious sounds
filling the land lips
cracked as the river bed.

BOOTS SIREECH [Ute]

My Son

Go, my son, and dance

Go and learn

Go and show those who laugh at you.
Go and dance among the beating sound of the war
     drums
Go and dance among the chanting voices,
those that chant by day and by night.

Yes, my son has danced
My son went and danced among the chanting voices
and among the beating of the war drums.

And now there is no one to laugh at my son.
There is no one left to tell how my son danced.
Where are they?
Where did they go?

Here we stand, facing the wind.
Here we stand, listening to the wind as it carries
     away
the sounds of the war drums.
Here shall the wind blow;
Here my son and I stand alone.

Soon only the wind will know my son.

RICHARD SMITH

Till Forever and More

i thought you and i would be friends
  forever
   until the sun died
   until the grass would grow no more

i let you go your way
  that was not enough

i trusted you
  before my heart was bleeding
  before my guts were torn
  before my thoughts scattered
  before the lands stolen
   the women and children dead
    the Circle of Life
     almost broken.

Hear me, america
still i live
  the memory of your lies
   fills my heart
  memories of The People's blood
   on your hands and lips
  the memory of your darkest
    white thoughts

Hear me america
  you can never be forgiven

Hear me america
you will never be forgiven

Hear me america

Never.

VICKIE VIGIL

Native Tongue

you with the funny sound to someone's ear
you that i understand
it's a welcome to hear you
you who is hardly known
even among your own people.
you who teaches me truth
coming from the heart.
the echo of our forefathers
you bring to us.
you speak from within.
my friend, native tongue,
i will not forget.

RAYMOND TEESETESKIE [Cherokee]

My Kind of School

Deep in the forest
Where a cool breeze
Fans my face,
Where the warm sun
Shines in bright
Geometry problems
Through the leaves
While birds lecture and scold
And squirrels play at recess
Through the trees—
This is my kind of school.

Or give me
A great rock ledge
Overlooking a valley.
Below me, let me study
People as they rush about
As if today stands alone—
Their only time
For running past
Their neighbors.
And still I sit
In quietness,
Learning from them
What to run
As to run,
As to run . . .

TEKAHIONWAKE [Mohawk]

The Cattle Thief

You have stolen my father's
   spirit, but his body I only claim.

You have killed him, but you
   shall not dare to touch him
   now he's dead.

You have cursed, and called
   him a Cattle Thief, though
   you robbed him first of bread.

Robbed him and robbed my
   people—look there, at that
   shrunken face,
Starved with a hollow hunger,
   we owe to you and your
   race.

What have you left to us of
   land, what have you left of
   game,

What have you brought but
   evil, and curses since you
   came?

How have you paid us for
   our game? How paid us for
   our land?

By a book, to save our souls

from the sins you brought
   in your other hand.

Go back with your new relig
   ion, we never have understood,

Your robbing an Indian's
   body, and mocking his soul with food.

Go back with your new re
   ligion, and find if you
   can,

The honest man you have ever
   made from out a starving man.

You say your cattle are not
   ours, your meat is not our
   meat;

When you pay for the land
   you live in, we'll pay for
   the meat we eat.

Give back our land and our
   country, give back our
   herds of game;

Give back the furs and the
   forests that were ours be
   fore you came;

Give back the peace and plen
  ty. Then come with your
  new belief,

And blame, if you dare, the
  hunger that drove him to
  be a thief.

EUGENE TSO

I Am Hungry

I was hungry and you
    landed on the moon.

I was hungry and you
    told me to wait.

I was hungry and you
    set up a commission.

I was hungry and you
    told me I shouldn't be.

I was hungry and you
    had missile bills to pay.

I was hungry and you said
    "Machines do that kind of work now."

I was hungry and you said
    "The poor are always with us."

was hungry and you said
   "Law and order come first."

was hungry and you said
   "Blame it on the Communists."

was hungry and you said
   "So were my ancestors."

was hungry and you said
   "We don't hire after 35."

was hungry and you said
   "God helps those. . . ."

was hungry and you said
   "Sorry, come back tomorrow."

TURTLE'S SON

Pyramid Lake 1970

A curved bow, white dots of fire crystals are the
    pelicans,
  skimming the surface of Pyramid Lake, following,
  it almost seems, their shadowed bow before them,
  as they fish and have fished since Coyote first
    fashioned
      this sacred lake.

(A broken line of hip-booted fishermen in grim
    determination,
  casting shoulder to shoulder for the trout born of
    hatcheries,
  returning yearly to this spot where they were
    dumped,
  seeking their mother warden with metal star,
    perhaps,
      intruders to this lake.)

The old man whose fingers fashion drums and
    arrows,
  who is and was forever the Paiute guardian of
    these waters,
  sings lonely as he walks the dunes which are his
    earth,
  sings lonely as he tans the buckskin for his
    grandson,
      who must dance eagles.

Indians of All Tribes who have come upon a raven's
    wing,
  white buffalo and deerskin people, totem pole,
    katchina and

and painters, hunters of the Everglades and
    ains and forests,
united under the Spirit sky to support their brother
        Paiutes
                this sacred lake to replenish.

the old man whose fingers fashion drums and
        arrows,
    who is and was forever the Paiute guardian of
        these waters,
    sings softly, ever softly of an All Tribes people,
        softly,
    sings a unity, to the sky, to earth, to sacred lake,
            sings softly, forever, forever.

GERALD ROBERT VIZENOR [Chippewa]

Haiku

        With the moon
My young father comes to mind
        Walking the clouds.

        Under the full moon
My shadow moves like a stranger
        First Autumn frost.

        Horse in the frost
Like an engine puffing the slopes
        Missing a breath.

        Early snow
Old woman on a park bench
        Smell of moth balls.

Drifting snow
Curls like the lips of a dog
Meeting a stranger.

Every day at the lake
Our footprints are washed away
Remembering a friend.

JAMES WELCH [Blackfeet]

Getting Things Straight

Is the sun the same drab gold?
The hawk—is he still rising, circling,
falling above the field? And the rolling day,
it will never stop? It means nothing?
Will it end the way history ended when
the last giant climbed Heart Butte, had his vision
came back to town and drank himself
sick? The hawk has spotted a mouse.
Wheeling, falling, stumbling to a stop;
he watches the snake ribbon quickly
under a rock. What does it mean?
He flashes his wings to the sun, bobs
twice and lifts, screaming
off the ground. Does it mean this to him:
the mouse, a snake, the dozen angry days
still rolling since his last good feed?
Who offers him a friendly meal?
Am I strangling in his grip?
Is he my vision?

TOM WHITECLOUD

Thief

We knew of war
For we were warriors
The winner takes all.

We knew of lies
For we were diplomats
in a small way.

We knew of politics,
for we were democrats:
a man was a man.

You took the land
We tried to understand;
You live on it, not with it.

But, my friends,
(And you were often good friends
As you understand friendship):

Why did you steal the smiles
From our children?

RAY YOUNG BEAR [Mesquaki]

Through Lifetime

white buffalo sleeping through snow and mixes
me into animal bones avoiding to be struck by
      daylight.

red colored evenings accepted the meat
thrown as offering over this man's old sky shoulders.
it seem that while he skinned his kill
songs formed from hard life of earthmaker
and he sat with knife eager for his wind
to carry body scent other directions.

there are in a house of many years
my shoulders held by fingers of the sun.
a mourning woman who sat in the middle
with rainwater eyes came as mother and wrapped
a red blanket over my ways and edges.

she combed my hair with wings of the seeking owl.
she sang of spring birds and how brown running
      waters
would be a signal to begin family deaths by
      witchcraft,
she showed me a handful of ribs shining a land day

i leaned too close to the sun and felt the warmth of
      peyote
pumping my blood.
i washed my face with thunder songs that touched
      low
and earth attached a vision to his long followers.
i listened to my sad hunting dogs tremble magically

of two crows chasing spirits away from
      fasting-ones.
i thought of an intended life and autumn came shyly
bearing songs but no gentle children.

woman of the horses sat in my circles.
she created fire burning only when bears cleaned the
      skin
of people from their teeth beside dreaming rivers.
the northern lights carried the meaning of life
far past the sufferings of night enemies.
old men inside rainbows offered no messages but
      whispered
of another existence closer to a prayer than tears

my raining-grandfathers walked speaking in choices
over the black skies.
i stood inside them and released my hand
which held my words gathered into parts of the
      earth.

Chicano
Poems

Introduction
RICARDO SÁNCHEZ

In poetry, as in his social life, the Chicano is exploring the core issues of what it means to survive while others thrive. The Chicano experience is as varied as those who live it; therefore, Chicano poetry is varied in perspective. But most Chicano poets do write in and around the central themes of hunger, poverty, identity crises, social abnegation, hope, *carnalismo* (a love/brotherhood), justice, *Chicanismo, machismo,* Aztlan and other social phenomena—all encompassed by the barrio experience. It is in the barrio language and in the life style of its inhabitants that the poetry of the Chicano takes on life and becomes an expletive that mirrors the Chicano's view of himself.

When the Chicano poet deals with the barrio, he invariably must deal with its extensions, which go beyond the physical context of the barrio—the experiences of *la pinta* (the joint/prison), escape into the military, the labyrinths of bureaucracy (national, state, local, university, government and industry). In essence, most Chicanos retain the feel and psychology of the barrio, for even those who have made it still respond with a *grito** in their moments of anomie and social abnegation. Mariachis and their music are a paradox within the soul-conscience of the Chicanos—an Elysian euphony to love and a lament of death and the dying of love. Similarly, poetry for most Chicanos—especially those in the movement—becomes a *grito:* an expression of liberation (*I am Chicano!*) and a serious questioning of the system (we are brutalized!).

The Chicano poet uses poetry to express conditions that do exist, do plague and do cripple the Chicano masses; he protests, expands on his hope and creates fleeting images of a world where the Chicano can and must be master of his own destiny. A transformation has come about in the barrios—the barrio Chicano has now become politicized and societally aware of all that is possible to him, if the society in which he survives becomes flexible enough to accord him his place. In

* outcry

the process, he has begun to articulate the poetry he has always felt, while rejecting a materialistic structure. The result, thus far, has been a self-affirmation, oftentimes a journeying to the very beginning of history in the Western Hemisphere; a poetic outlet for sublimating the realities of social frustration, abnegation and anomie. The Chicano poet, instead of writing graffiti on the barrio walls, now pens questions and hopes, and in this is poetically demanding a serious response from the society he still views as a system bent on his annihilation or assimilation.

Chicano writers perforce are activists with racial/ethnic social mandates. Within the mandate for the creation of a new literature is the unspoken command to bring about an understanding of the language. Chicano language is like all languages in transition—the merging of other languages and social influences. It is in the merging of human diversity that we can see growth and humanistic evolvement. A correct language is one that communicates—and within its communicativeness, it should grow and develop—not only new words, but new ways to express the worlds of language we live in. So it is with Chicano literature—Español and English merging as a base to create another apex of human expression.

We are a new people, but not in the sense that we just sprang up. We are a new people because we have just recently begun to define our humanity through our own art forms and social interpretations within the mass media. By our own definitions shall we be known, not by the sly or off-handed characterizations of Anglo sociologists out to make a name for themselves. Because a new generation of Chicanos has determined that we will be the ones to determine our own destinies, because we have begun to reexamine all social conditioning, because we are recording the reality of the Chicano, it can now be said that there is indeed a new people that is stamping its name on history.

It is sad to realize that of all the hundreds of thousands of various groups of people who have existed, we know only of those who created art forms that lived on beyond them. Man's history and his evolution have an infinity of anonymous pages, for man's need for survival is sometimes so great he cannot afford the time nor the luxury of writing/painting out his reality. Fortunately for us, Chicanos have now begun to write Chicano history and literature, and in the process share the many-sided realities of *la vida* with all who care to further mankind's humanistic trajectory.

As the hopes of a people build up, new worlds come into focus, and the words of first creation link together past and present. Chicano literature keeps time to the beat of many drums. It is not only about poverty; it is not only about hurt and the socialization process, but rather about all the human and social needs of *La Raza*.* Need is not confined to the physical; it is also spiritual—the quality that can be found wherever and whenever a human being poses questions on the why of existence. Our literature is humorous, for our lives reek with *cabula,* Chicano jive. It is serious; it is built on hope and love; it exists.

* The Mexican-American people

ALURISTA

Mis ojos hinchados

Mis ojos hinchados
    flooded with lágrimas
de bronce
melting on the cheek bones
of my concern
    razgos indígenas
the scars of history on my face
    and the veins of my body
that aches
    vomito sangre
y lloro libertad
    I do not ask for freedom
I *am* freedom
    no one
not even Yahweh
    and his thunder
can pronounce
    and on a stone
la ley del hombre esculpir
    no puede
mi libertad
and the round tables

Mis ojos hinchados: my swollen eyes
lágrimas de bronce: brass tears
razgos indígenas: native (Indian) features
vomito sangre: I vomit blood
y lloro libertad: and I weep for liberty
la ley del hombre esculpir no puede: he cannot engrave the law of
    man
mi libertad: my freedom

    of ice cream
        hot dog
    meat ball lovers meet
to rap
    and rap
and I hunger
    y mi boca está seca
el agua cristalina
    y la verdad
  transparent
in a cup
    is never poured
dust gathers on the shoulders
    of dignitaries
y de dignidad
    no saben nada
muertos en el polvo
    they bite the earth
and return
    to dust

---

y mi boca está seca: and my mouth is dry
el agua cristalina: the crystal water
y la verdad: and truth
y de dignidad no saben nada: and they know nothing of dignity
muertos en el polvo: dead in the dust

JORGE ALVAREZ

Autobiography in Maize

I am a Quetzal
Who wakes up green
With wings of gold
And cannot fly;

I am the ear
Of Epictetus
Written on the Roman lash,
While the Sundays bring
The black-shawled hundreds
To the fore;

I am the stiff volcano
Sitting on grey hair,
And mangled hands
Pull up the hod
To start another day;

I am the candle
Under images in empty rooms
Where bare feet
Paint mosaics
On the moon;

I am the parachute
Painted
On the Aztec risers
Leading to the sky;

I am the book
Torn sideways in despair

To drop the image
Of an old man
Dancing in the square;

I am the eye
Of a small child
With stains of corn
Upon his teeth;

I am the dark horizon
Of old homes
And the Quetzal
He will someday see.

MARINA DE BELLAGENTE

I am the land. I wait.

I am the land. I wait.
You say you own me.
I wait.

You shout. I lie patient.
You buy me. I wait.
With muddy holes and
car lot eyes I stare . . .
    Then someone
tickles me, plants life—fruit
grass—trees/ children dance/ someone
    Sings

You come with guns
A chainlink necklace
chokes me now

I wait.
YOU CANNOT PUT A FENCE
AROUND THE PLANET EARTH.
I am the land. I wait.

RENÉ CÁRDENAS

La muerte del Sr. Durán

"¿Es usted uno de los Buenos?"
was the first he ever spoke to me.
Have I or we ever known if we are from the Best?
Do we aspire for God's best,
Man's best even?
¿O qué?

El Sr. Durán asked me for my patronym—
all names are great in Mexico—
and had known some good ones . . .
Have we ever known some good ones? Good
men for us to be with, their sons or daughters?
"¿Es usted uno de los Buenos?"
was the last he ever spoke to me.
Soy Chicano: I am the best, but not of Duran's
Good Ones. *¿Y tu?*
Soon after I saw him at the hospital, drawn and
        unrelenting
(like a caged eagle inside that cancer-ripped frame),
in church an usher handed me a hymn
sheet in Spanish. I looked at him in surprise and he
motioned, saying softly, *"Hay hágale no más, que
        li'ase."* So I
sang a little—the hell with them.

¿Es usted uno de los Buenos?: Are
    you one of the good ones?
¿O qué?: or what?
El Sr. Durán: Mr. Duran
Soy Chicano: I am a Chicano

¿Y tu?: and you?
*Hay hágale no más, que
    li'ase:* Just fake it, what
    does it matter.

Así el Sr. Durán
living for what he wanted:
they say that he was a sucker for hungry bums,
migrant workers, deadbeat winos who came
to his restaurant—
he gave five dollars and fifty cents worth
of lunch tickets for promises never turned to
gold. He was a good one for Chicanos.
In the last year he played a mental chess
game *con la calavera;* he was living because
he wanted to.

He had no head for business, he ran the world
to suit himself—you didn't have to know him.
The revolution brought him to Arizona—
he had pesos in a glass jar to pay his land
taxes, he raised tall sons and daughters.
I saw him when he was finally letting go,
telling death to go to hell,
dying because he wanted to.
And the last thing he ever said
of all the best things he ever said,
of the Revolution y la Chicanada—
"¿Es usted uno de los Buenos?"

Así el Sr. Durán: and so Mr. Duran
con la calavera: with the (his) skull

ABELARDO DELGADO

Icon

the mariachi, esterophonized
made me realize
that sundays in el paso,
los angeles and denver
are a very lonely thing,
they have a way of erasing
church people until you
are alone with the marble
and wooden statues
and the color t.v.
with o.j.simpson
running and namath throwing
is dark even when on
and restaurants become
peopleless
where you order your breakfast
through a microphone
and it comes
through an aluminum door
and all of a sudden
you also realize
that for the brevity
of a deep breath
you no longer have a wife,
children, father, mother,
brothers or friends
or lovers . . .
and your plain pale blue shirt
has yesterday's sweat
and the rug
under your feet
is soft

but you have taken off
and the chest pains
you had as you inhaled
blend with the
hazy sunday
in the middle of september
a picture of god you cannot help remember. . . .

ANTHONY D'ESPOSITO

In Five Hundred Years

My father hunted the great mammoth
And I am only five hundred years old
Who can still remember the blood of Montezuma
And the crying at Wounded Knee

And I am only five hundred years old
Who yesterday was herded on a trail of tears
And a hundred Sand Creeks flow
Through veins my Indian heart feeds

And I am only five hundred years old
And my dream is just now beginning
As the drums of "Unity" throb by spirit
And all of the people do a round dance

And our Mother Earth is in round dance
And all the stars circle our eagle dream
And the children of Aztlan run and play
I'm glad to be a youth of only five hundred years

ESTUPINIAN

In Our House

Smells
like endless strings
of *chorizos*
squirm from the past
and we sort them
from sounds
from sweet-smelling orange juice
puddles on oil cloth
". . . *el niño necesita zapatos*"
stick from morning and . . .

"*Saca la guitarra* . . ."
and we lay in beds
damp . . . damn coldness
smell damp
"*y que siga la parranda* . . ."
my brother's feet are cold
like a pup's nose
"*y que bonito canta Ines!*"
like the smell
of orange juice puddles
like endless strings
of Agustin Lara
and strings of *chorizos*.

---

chorizos: Spanish-type sausages
el niño necesita zapatos: the boy
    needs shoes
saca la guitarra: take the guitar

y que siga la parranda: the fun
    should continue
y que bonito canta Ines: and how
    lovely is Ines's singing

MANUEL CHAVARRIA FLORES

Indian, You Travel

Indian, you travel all the roads of America,
Sometimes over peaks that rise from the earth
and break through the blue curve of heaven
to peer at infinity;
Sometimes through the lands that burn
You with the fire of the tropics;
Your feet mount the roads of weariness
You water the distances
With the sweat of your brown muscles;
You still carry on your dark backs
the cacaxtle, the crate, of burdens
Laid upon you by Pedro de Alvarado, the
      Conquistador.

Listen to me:
I, too, am Indian,
Another man of your race,
Another son of America
Who travels along the roads of my life,
Roads sometimes steep, harsh, and difficult,
Sometimes level, but rough and wearisome,
And I anoint my road with rebellion,
Sweating I hold tight infinite anxieties
And I carry my load of anguish
Of hopes and dreams
On the numbed back of my soul.

Indian, let us trade our burdens,
Perhaps your crate of roasting stones,
Of big jars and fruits,
Is not so heavy
As the enormous load I carry on my soul.

UAN GARCIA

My People

Just as lightning that rips
apart a tree so deeply
embedded in the earth

My people have the strength
to rip apart this cruel system
that subjects us since our birth
Like the winds that tear through
the mountain peaks so cold so high.

My people will tear through this
society that has nothing to offer
but its lies.

Like the power of the sun
that radiates and makes things grow

The power of our strength
will break through the bondage
that destroys us so.

Unlike this system that creates
a world of fantasy to keep
from seeing the truth

My people will be the light
that man saw first when
he was earth's fruit
Not like the corruption that

permeates in the minds of men
fat and blown.

My people are the flowers
and the blossoms of the
earth not yet full grown.

LUIS GARCIA

The Cage

Someone is turning lips of gold
into ditches of blood
millions of dollars
are falling in love
with a coffin.

The eggs of suicide
hatching thousands of corpses
nourish
one jungle after another.

Screaming leaves
and the smoke from villages
that never quit burning
invade the eyes of oblivion.

Let's try to imitate
the voice of an umbrella
says a clown to the people
who know that living
can be a gentle game.

A candle of tears
with the voice of a lemon exclaims

he violets in your grandmother's garden
re my cousins.

n angel who makes windows that fly
nd inhabits an elevator
t the bottom of a lake
nelts a chain
vith the voice he keeps
n the bones of his fingers.

o it all comes down to this—
a voice that doesn't exist
xcept when the door of a cage
s accidentally left open.

MANUEL GOMEZ

We Are Beautiful!

BEGINNING
THE RED SUN'S
SWORD SLASHES
MY SOUL
AND BLACK BLOOD
FLOWS FROM MY DARKNESS
I AM THE SON OF AN
ANCIENT PEOPLE
MY POEMS ARE MY TEARS
TEARS OF BLOOD
AND FIRE

RODOLFO GONZALES

from I Am Joaquin

I am Joaquin,
Lost in a world of confusion,
Caught up in a whirl of an
      Anglo society,
Confused by the rules,
Scorned by attitudes,
Suppressed by manipulations,
And destroyed by modern society.
My fathers
  have lost the economic battle
and won
  the struggle of cultural survival.
And now!
  I must choose
       Between
  the paradox of
Victory of the spirit,
despite physical hunger
       Or
  to exist in the grasp
of American social neurosis,
sterilization of the soul
  and a full stomach.

Yes,
I have come a long way to nowhere,
Unwillingly dragged by that
  monstrous, technical
  industrial giant called
      Progress

d Anglo success . . .
I look at myself.
   I watch my brothers.
      I shed tears of sorrow.
         I sow seeds of hate.
I withdraw to the safety within the
ircle of life . . .
         MY OWN PEOPLE . . .

have endured in the rugged mountains
   of our country
have survived the toils and slavery
   of the fields.
         I have existed
a the barrios of the city,
n the suburbs of bigotry,
n the mines of social snobbery,
n the prisons of dejection,
n the muck of exploitation
nd
n the fierce heat of racial hatred.

And now the trumpet sounds,
The music of the people stirs the
         Revolution,
Like a sleeping giant it slowly
rears its head
to the sound of
            Tramping feet
            Clamouring voices
            Mariachi strains
         Fiery tequila explosions
      The smell of chile verde and
      Soft brown eyes of expectation for a
                  better life.

And in all the fertile farm lands,
                    the barren plains,
the mountain villages,
smoke smeared cities
            We start to MOVE.
  La Raza!
Mejicano!
  Español!
    Latino!
      Hispano!
        Chicano!
or whatever I call myself,
            I look the same
            I feel the same
            I cry
                and
            Sing the same

I am the masses of my people and
I refuse to be absorbed.
            I am Joaquin
The odds are great
but my spirit is strong
                My faith unbreakable
                My blood is pure
I am Aztec Prince and Christian Christ
            I SHALL ENDURE!
            I WILL ENDURE!

GRAFFITTI

7th Street

When I walk down
our street
I am afraid
I am afraid
not of the meager lights
or of the boys
    grown old before their time . . .

But of the white helmets
that hold lead-weighted night sticks
that prod and poke and irritate
till a red film runs over my eye
until I am forced to strike . . .

Too late, too late to stop
for now I will wake up
hurt and bruised all over
leaving a spasm of pain
not through my body
but through my soul . . .

Where in a Chicano
it hurts most of all ·

For now
when I go down the street
I will no longer be afraid
for when I go down
one will be below me
and one above . . .

Only then, in the other land
will I stand
and be counted
among the people
LA RAZA

JOSÉ ANGEL GUTIERREZ

22 miles

From 22 I see my first 8 weren't.
  Around the 9th, I was called "meskin,"
    By the 10th, I knew and believed I was.
      I found out what it meant to know, to believe
      . . . before my 13th.

Through brown eyes, seeing only brown colors and
    feeling only
brown feelings . . . I saw . . . I felt . . . I hated . . . I
    cried . . . I tried
. . . I didn't understand during these 4.
                I rested by just giving up.

While, on the side . . . I realized I *believed* in
white as pretty,
my being governor
  blond blue-eyed baby Jesus,
    cokes and hamburgers
      equality for all regardless of race, creed, or
        color,
      Mr. Williams, our banker.
      I had to!
      That was all I had.

Beams and Communism were bad.
                    Past the weeds, atop the hill, I
                        looked back.

Pretty people, combed and squeaky clean, on
        arrowlike roads.
Pregnant girls, ragged brats, swarthy machos, rosary
        beads,
and friends waddle clumsily over and across hills,
        each other,
mud, cold, and woods on caliche ruts.
    At the 19th mile, I fought blindly at everything and
        anything.
        Not knowing, Not caring about WHY, WHEN, or
            FOR WHAT.
            I fought. And fought.
                By the 21st, I was tired and tried.

                    But now . . .
I've been told that I am dangerous.
That is because I am good at not being a Mexican.
That is because I know now that I have been cheated.
That is because I hate circumstances and love
        choices.

    You know . . . chorizo tacos y tortillas ARE good,
            even at school.
    Speaking Spanish is a talent.
Being Mexican IS as good as Rainbo bread.
And without looking back, I know that there are still
        too many
    brown babies,
        pregnant girls,
            old 25-year-old women,
                drunks,
                    who should have lived but didn't,

on those caliche ruts.

It is tragic that my problems during these
      past 21 miles were/are/might be . . .
  looking into blue eyes,
   wanting to touch a gringita,
 ashamed of being Mexican,
believing I could not make it at college,
pretending that I liked my side of town,

   remembering the Alamo,
  speaking Spanish in school bathrooms only
and knowing that Mexico's prostitutes like
    Americans better.

At 22, my problems are still the same but now I know
    I am your
problem
That farm boys, Mexicans and Negro boys are in
    Vietnam is but one
thing I think about:
          Crystal City, Texas 78839
          The migrant worker;
          The good gringo:

Staying Mexican enough;
Helping;
Looking at the world from the back of a truck.

The stoop labor with high school rings on their
    fingers;
The Anglo cemetery,
Joe the different Mexican,
     Damn.
     Damn.
     Damn.

JOHN FELIPE HERRERA

A Certain Man

The man over there
with educated fingers and fast
    clouds
around his flag
rolls his shirt sleeves & calls
a taxi from church . . .
His eyeteeth clap like his family
for an encore of southwest earth
wolfed with fever
. . . . Skilled and styled to believe
that Moctezuma blood & spirit
. . . . are dead, as he pumps
a book through his ears.
Inside his stomach
roast meat (buttered in
    philosophy)
makes yellow drops
on his hide overboil down
to his buttons.
Only heavy fur pulls
his head to a pillow
rusting completely overnight
. . . . like his prayer.

Moctezuma: the Mexicans use this spelling rather than
"Montezuma."

DONNA JAMES

Cresciendo en el barrio

Cresciendo en el barrio
Muriendo en las calles
La historia de la Raza
De la gente brava

     And so they grow—the little brown babies
     From hope to hate

     I

     A flash/of excitement
     As the iron monsters roar by
     And the vino flows freely
     At the eternal street corner party
     "Madre de dios, estoy un poco high."

     2

     And the gringo comes down to the barrio
     To buy piñatas y dulces

Cresciendo en el barrio: growing up in the barrio
Muriendo en las calles: dying in the streets
La historia de la Raza: the history of the people (*La Raza* refers to
    the Mexicans as an ethnic-cultural entity.)
De la gente brava: of the (brave, angry, wild) people; *bravo, (a)* has
    all these meanings.
vino: wine
Madre de dios, estoy un poco high: Mother of God, I am a little
    high
piñatas y dulces: Piñata is a Mexican clay jug filled with goodies;
    it is broken by the children in a game. *Dulces* are sweets.

And comment on the filth
Of our unswept, child littered streets
"How can they live that way Henry
When personal hygiene is so basic?"

3

Saturday night/with nothing but reds
Sit on the sidewalk and dream

4

And in the clinics niños die
Before and after birth
"Far too many Mexicans in this town"
"Don't they breed like rabbits though/"

5

They go to school, we go to school y
          aprendemos nada
Because there is nothing for us to learn
The street has taught us all/
Made us worldly wise
Survival by example, not by book

---

niños: children
aprendemos nada: we learn nothing

6

Y los hermanos look around
Learn of Che, Sandino, Villa
Find our culture is not standing
But running swiftly forward
A revolutionary spirit kills no friends

And so the babies grow
From hope to righteous hate

La historia de la Raza
De la gente brava
Luchando para vivir
Viviendo para luchar

Y los hermanos: and the brothers
Luchando para vivir: fighting in order to live
Viviendo para luchar: living in order to fight

Untitled [sin titulo]

Dirty little Mexican!
  Dirty little Mexican!
—¿Por que me odian tanto papa?
—¿Por que me odian tanto mama?
  walked to school, miles to school
What a fool fool fool
                FOOL!
Stupid little Mexican,
         So long ago. . . . in school.

—Hijito, te peliates otra vez. Cómo me
  Duele tanto verte peliando en las calles.
—Si, mama, si, mamacita.
Como le duele tanto a una madre.

—HO! We have a very good shop program, Pancho.
—You are so skillful with your hands.
         Go to trade school!
             GO TO TRADE SCHOOL!
                (fool)

¿Por que me odian tanto papa?: Why do they hate me so, Papa?
Hijito, te peliates otra vez. Cómo me duele tanto verte
peliando en las calles: Little son, you've been fighting again. How it
    hurts me to see you fighting in the streets.
Si, mama, si, mamacita. Como le duele tanto a una madre: Yes,
    Mama, yes, little mama. How it hurts a mother.

—Mira mamacita te hice una lamparita.
—Mira papa te hice un "stand" para tus pipas.

—Que bueno es m'hijo.
Lamps for mama—many lamps
Mom still has them.
Pipe racks for papa
Papa never smoked a pipe.

　Dear Mom and Dad,
Cómo estraño el amor de mis padres aquí.
　Today I finished boot camp, mama. Tomorrow
we get our orders. I expect to get into radio
school because I did so good in the test
　　　　　　　　Love
　　　　　　　　　Your son

González
Pérez
Ramírez
López
　　　　F.M.F.
　　　　　Infantry
　　　　　　VIETNAM!

_____

Mira mamacita te hice una lamparita: Look, Mama, I made you a
　little lamp.
Mira papa te hice un "stand" para tus pipas: Look, Papa, I made
　you a stand for your pipes.
Que bueno es m'hijo: How good our son is.
Cómo estraño el amor de mis padres aquí: How I miss my parents'
　love here.

Jones, radio school
Smith, radar school

Hijo
Como nos da tristesa que estas tan lejos de nosotros.
Reso todos los dias por ti. Tu papa no a podido
    travajar
mucho esta semana por las lluvias. Cuidate hijo
              Tu Madre y Padre
              Que te quieren mucho.

—I'm sorry, sir, we don't have anything for unskilled
    workers.
—May I suggest you go to the farm labor office.
—They are always looking for workers.
            MIERDA!
—Hey, Punk, come over here. —No Sir.
—Hay, Punk, Where is your I.D. —No officer.
—Hay, Mex, Smoking any marihuana lately? —No,
    Pig.
—Hay, Chicano, Get your hands over your head. —No
—No Pinch! Chango Cabrón

      Basta Basta Bastardo
        YA BASTA!

Hijo, como nos da tristesa que estas tan lejos de nosotros: Son, how
    sad it makes us that you are so far from us.
*Reso todos los dias por ti. Tu papa no a podido travajar mucho
    esta semana por las lluvias. Cuidate hijo. Tu Madre y Padre
    que te quieren mucho:* I pray every day for you. Your father
    could not work much this week because of the rain. Take care
    of yourself, son. Your father and mother who love you very
    much.
Mierda: shit
Chango: monkey
Cabrón: he-goat, cuckold
Basta: enough
Bastardo: bastard

M. JUNGE

Upon Submitting Proposals
for Federally Funded Summer Programs

You and I. We know
Each other well,
We are dealers
in important words,
Dabblers in heavy concepts.
We meet to flick
Our tongues deliciously
Across profound ideas.
We nod and smile.
We understand.

So spring comes again
and like a lover gone
Mad with meaning,
I send you solemnly
This year's ponderous supply
Of words.
Neatly typed
and double spaced
That you asked me for.
And couched in poetry.

I send you a poem of poverty's wars.
I sing of jobs and work experiences
And training for disadvantaged
And deprived and disenfranchised youth
With grass or other kinds of roots
From impacted areas of inner cities
And ghettos and barrios
To help their self-images and self-concepts
And give them growth experiences

That are meaningful and creative
and life-changing
WOWIE—ZOWIE—ZAP!!!

You respond pleasantly enough
in triplicate. Asking only
That I fill out
One million count them
important forms in quadruplicate
Mailing each one to fifteen different
important persons, sitting in 63 different
Offices, taking hundreds of days
Calling themselves bureaucrats
Who as we all know
Are the keepers of the red tape

And you will send me post haste
By return mail, if not sooner,
The bread.

But I know a sweet-faced young dude
in blue knit cap
With paint on his nostrils from
Sniffing and on his jacket
Who writes his name on
My house and still high
Steals the battery out of my car
Because mistakenly he thinks
It will run his stolen tape deck.
Who does not ever go to school
And thus cannot achieve the lofty
Rank of dropout.
The invisible man all too visible

By his acts
Known mostly to the guys at juvie and camp
But not to his own mother.

And one thing bothers me:
What does that young dude know
Of our important words? What does he
Care for our heavy concepts? What can even
Our bread do for the
Already too enduringly human quality
Of his all too personal
And almost-over life?

DIANA LOPEZ

Sestina: Santa Prisca

One would think that these
Dry standards of pink stone
Would whip the wind with iron
Tongues and speak the word
Kept by their chiseled, gesticulating saints
Weeping dust tears upon the courtyard floor.

From the chequered, knee-rubbed floor
Rise supplications cast with wings of iron
To perch with gentle claws upon the word
"God" carved with gold upon the pimpled stone.
Futile as this chasuble of rock, these
Prayers can never tame the gestures of the saints.

Now the sun strikes with glory the cold saints
Forcing their lips to simulate a word

Voiced to silver by the bells of iron.
Each note a silver globule floats to crack these
Shallow crystals of the morning hours lying on the
     floor
And scatter their potions of tranquility on the stone.

It is not time for winds to ruffle the starched stone
Which clothes the rock-ribbed bosoms of the saints
And checks the pulses of the word.
It will never be time to resuscitate these
Dead theologies groveling on the vestry floor
Rehearsing one-time truths from vellums bound in
     iron.

The lacework of the sun-forged iron
Is not wide enough to let the saints
Escape wearing their still phylacteries of stone.
The bougainvillaea climbs its progress from the floor
To leave its purple kisses on the saints' lips; these
Let the bits of passion drop, but keep the precious
     word.

But it is there, the tongue-tied word
Encapsuled in its throats of iron,
To shake to truth the rock-hinged saints
Hanging like dead murmurs above the ocean floor.
The matutinal orations will rise on plumes of stone
And the loud tongues of candles whisper: "Listen to
     these."

The bells of iron will testify their love and these
Flowers on the floor become testaments from which
     the saints
Will preach the golden word and the green life-stone.

GABRIEL O. LOPEZ

Doing Time

When you dream of girls and wake
up leaning against cold steel
      You're doing time

When you hate the ring of a bell
with a passion
      You're doing time

  When you jump out of bed, use
  the toilet and wash your face
  without taking another step
      You're doing time

When you watch seasons flash
by your window
      You're doing time

  When you write letters and can't
  think of what to say
      You're doing time

When your room only has forty
square feet of floor space
      You're doing time

When you start looking and
feeling old
      You've done time.

RAMÓN MARTINEZ

Cow Comes Home

"After nine years, cow finally
comes home,"
read the local paper's
headlines.

Where did you go,
Bossy?
Why did you come
home?

Didn't you like the
billboards
on the freeways as you sped
away?

And surely you were
pleased
by the spics at that drive-in
theatre.

Did you run back
home
Because you didn't like
John Wayne's face?

Or did the nice
drunk
stop feeding you all the peanut-butter cups
he had?

Did you miss the

blue-eyed
farmer, with his machine washable
wife?

Tell me, Bossy, when your
parade
ended, were you
glad?

When your old bones
carried you
into the old
pasture,

Tell me, Bossy, as you
smiled,
did the farmer
cry?

JOSÉ MONTOYA

Sunstruck While Chopping Cotton

It was at first a single image.
A mirage-like illusional dance
Wavering and decomposing in the
Distance like a plastic mosaic.

Then it cleared.

Not one but three Bothisattvas
Suspended in a cloud of yellow dust
Just above the rows of cotton
Galloping comically on skeletal mounts

Across the arid, sponge-like lust
Of a desiccated desert.

They ride by, shouting in ruthless unison
The name of Jesus, across the valley
Halting not for an instant in their trek
To the distant sea.

The cool sea.

With flame throwers for nostrils
Their horses flee
Abreast the three
Halting whole freeways of awe-stricken traffic
And scattering chattering choppers
Welcoming the enormous episode as an excuse
For frolic fanfare.

They enter the sea and immediately get
cut down by surfboards sharp as razors
And oil-well derricks entangle them
And the horses, not being divine, drown.
And the Bothisattvas, mountless in the mire
Choke and struggle, making the Longbeach waters
Thick with blood, mud and crude oil.

But they are determined, and they walk
Nimbly and bloodied on the cracked-mirror
Surface with all the humility of the East
Then they forget and break into a run
Leaving bloodied footprints upon the blue waters,
Running, running toward the setting sun

Shouting, Jesus saves!
In ruthless unison.

ORLANDO ORTIZ

Reflections of an Inarticulate Childhood

the caves were lit
by faces drawn
in a hazy pose
of urined dreams,
through the summer air
my drumbeat rang
like carousels of sound,
I heard and danced
a savage dance
knife gleams at my feet,
you saw me run
over naked glass
eyes biting in the sun
a wolf-child speed
of rocks and bricks
as windows shattered gleaming sticks
gaping mouths exploding water,
gushed my skin, aware almost
of what it felt.
i bathed the flesh
of my animal self
alive to the instinct
of closing death
white in law
and in fact
the old woman who bore me
came to terms
and a kind of peace,
but i ran to touch and seek
what must be there

ebon skin woman
she rattled the eyes
on loose summer days
when children clank
with shoes of tin
and sweepers push
against the noonday tar.
whoring games of youthful play
were sweated august days,
the first surprising touch
and mystery thereof grew
moistened by her warmth
and swelling visions
on summer beds
played flaming walls
of rounded flesh
across the bricklike
prison of your mind,
you felt the need
to taste her flesh
and swim your head afire
across her chest
and pause reflect
upon the rising bone
and curve of shoulder warmth,
to reach her nervous thighs
engulfed in vaginal smiles
knowing her blackness
and your fantasy,
bitch of sensua

GUADALUPE de SAAVEDRA

IF You Hear that a Thousand People Love You

IF you hear that a thousand people love you
remember . . . saavedra is among them.

IF you hear that a hundred people love you
remember . . . saavedra is either in the first
              or very last row

IF you hear that seven people love you
remember . . . saavedra is among them,
like a wednesday in the middle of the week

IF you hear that two people love you
remember . . . one of them is saavedra

IF you hear that only one person loves you
remember . . . he is saavedra

AND when you see no one else around you,
      and you find out,
      that no one loves you anymore,
      then you will know for certain
       that . . . saavedra is dead

Aztec Angel

I

I am an Aztec angel
 criminal
  of a scholarly
   society
   I do favors
    for whimsical
     magicians
    where I pawn
     my heart
      for truth
    and find
     my way
    through obscure
     streets
      of soft spoken
   hara-kiris

II

I am an Aztec angel
 forlorn passenger
  on a train
  of chicken farmers
   and happy children

III

I am the Aztec angel
 fraternal partner
  of an orthodox
   society

where pachuca children
hurl stones
through poetry rooms
and end up in a cop car
their bones itching
and their hearts
busted from malnutrition

IV

I am the Aztec angel
who frequents bars
spends evenings
with literary circles
and socializes
with spiks
niggers and wops
and collapses on his way
to funerals

V

Drunk
lonely
bespectacled
the sky
opens my veins
like rain
clouds go berserk
around me
my Mexican ancestors
chew my fingernails
I am an Aztec angel
offspring
of a woman
who was beautiful

RICARDO SÁNCHEZ

Introduction to Abelardo

we shall joke and carry on til eternity freezes
over; we shall work late at night trying to sensi-
ze a frigid amerika, and our sweat shall drown
us . . . still it has been worth it, carnal, knowing
your madness and your sometimes off the wall
responses—for even in your jests you are deathly
serious . . . so serious that you are a measurable
menace to those who prefer not to think . . . write
on, carnal, or rejo in our minds and souls; in-
volve humanity in your quest for freedom—for
even a quixote like you can have the soul of el cid
and cuauhtemoc . . . carve your feelings on the
bosom of this bitching country, that truth might
prevail . . .

out of the holocaust that seems imminent,
beneath the atomic strewn rubble, beyond the
racist idiocy of this selfish country let your po-
etry prevail—a beacon guiding lost souls to a
possible salvation . . .

be that purgative that will clean out the rancid-
ness from the gaping bowels of amerika.

you are free enough, abelardo, to write realisti-
cally about your hurts and lacks—realistic
enough to accept your own human frailty . . .
realistic enough to only demand that humanity

---

carnal: blood brother
rejo: spike (also, figuratively, strength)

be human—and not for a machinistic plasticity
that can only react racistly . . .

this is how I view you, compa, from the coils
of my own brand of idiocy. . . .

HUGO STANCHI

To Buss's Grandma

Black Mother
who held my colored daughter's pink hand
and whispered ancient knowledge of times past into
her ear;
Black Mother
with hands of pearl
and rubber-sandaled feet
that trod the day-to-day living rooms,
where at last
people stand and stare
and silently bow
as they fade
into the fabric
of the empty shells
of their collective soul,
Black Mother—
I thank you.

---

compa: dialect for *compadre,*
i.e., landsman, compatriot

LUIS TALAMANTEZ

from (Reflections) of a Convict

WEBS OF LAST NIGHT'S SLEEP   SLIP AWAY
          FROM MY DRY EYES
AS THE NOISES INCREASE AROUND ME
I FEEL THE CHILL OF DECEMBER
ON MY NAKED BODY AND
      I REACH BLINDLY
FOR MY FALLEN BLANKETS THAT I LIFT
FROM THE CELL'S COLD FLOOR AND
        I THINK
   OF THE DAY AHEAD
WITH A SIMILAR THEME AS IN MY DREAMS
WHERE ANYTHING COULD HAPPEN
     ANYTHING MIGHT COME LOOSE.
   AND OF THINGS TO DO . . . . . . HERE
SO THAT BOREDOM WILL NOT OVERCOME ME
SO THAT TIME WILL GO ON
     FOR ONE MORE DAY

JUST A DAY AT A TIME
     IS ALL I ATTEMPT
        AT ONE TIME. . . . . NOW.

THIS DAY WILL BE A LONG ONE
       IT IS CHRISTMAS
I STILL CAN WONDER AT WHAT
     THIS MEX BOY
IS DOING HERE IN THIS WRONG PLACE

MY MOTHER
    SHE DID NOT TELL ME
        OF THESE PLACES
BUT
    SHE DID NOT HAVE NO CHANCE TO
        EITHER
        OR
MAYBE SHE THOUGHT HER HIJO WOULD NEVER
        FIND HIS WAY HERE. . . .
    WHEN I HEAR FROM MY AGED ABUELA
    WHO HAS TAKEN HER PLACE
SHE ASKS
    IF I AM COLD? BUT
SHE DOES NOT MEAN IF
    I HAVE ENOUGH CLOTHES
        OR A COAT
SHE IS OLD AND WRINKLED
    AND SHE IS WISE
        SHE HAS KNOWN
        HERSELF
THE WAYS OF THE PALE FOREIGNERS
IN OUR LAND AND WAY OF LIFE
    ALWAYS
  THE BRINGERS OF OUR TROUBLES
    THE INQUISITORS
BECKONING TO US WITH THEIR CROOK'D FINGERS
THEIR REDNECKS AND PANZAS SWOLLEN
        WITH POISONS
OF GREED AND CONSUMPTION

---

hijo: son
abuela: grandmother
panzas: bellies

CALLING US TO COME
           TO THEM
TO BE ABUSED, USED, AND SCREWED
    "WHATCHA GOT INDA BAG KID—
    WHAT'D YA GREASY FINGAS BEEN OUT
           STEALING NOW?"
"EET IS ONLY MY LUNCH FOR SCHOOL MEESTER"
I'VE REPLIED SO MANY TIMES IN THE PAST
IT WAS NOT ENOUGH
  THAT THEY HAD TAKEN GRANMA'S SONS AWAY
           TO WAR
BUT THEY'VE TAKEN HER GRANDSONS
           TO JAIL
SHE
  MI ABUELA STILL ASKS ME
IF MY HEART IS HEAVY TO BE FREE
    YES

        SI   SI   SI   SI   SI   SI   SI
      IT IS HEAVY——MUCHO
        IT IS MOSTLY ALSO
          EMPTY
           NOW
NO ONE WOULD THINK TO CONVINCE GRANMA THAT
        THE AMERICANO
DID NOT TAKE HER SON AWAY
        LONG AGO
JUST TO LEAVE HIM FAR AWAY . . . ON
      IWO JIMA
        A SPECK OF LAND
        NOT HIS OWN
SO THAT SHE NEVER SAW HIM AGAIN
  JUST A DEAD MEX

---

si: yes
mucho: very

ON A SPECK

WHAT THE HECK!

BUT NO ONE LAUGHS

BUT I REMEMBER WHEN GRANMA CRIED SILENTLY . . .

NOW NO ONE CAN TELL HER THAT

THE AMERICANO

DOES NOT HAVE HER NIETO

PRISONER

HURTING HIM SILENTLY AS OUR PEOPLE

HAVE LEARNED

TO BE HURT

KEEPING HIM

SO THAT SHE MAY NEVER SEE HIM AGAIN

EITHER

YET

HERE IN MY OWN HEART

THE WILL TO LIVE

LIVES ON

QUE TE PASA ABUELITA?

I AM ALWAYS HUNGRY NOW

MY HUNGER

AND THE YEARN TO BE FREE

WILL NEVER

DIE

---

nieto: grandson
que te pasa abuelita?: what is
    happening to you, dear grandmother?

GRE

Venture

behold, to be told
re or less in an ancient scroll
stranger in a lost paradise,
here no man ventures to be wise
e whiting burning in Egypt of all has no demands,
e buried race of the chariots,
e ages pass without a trace of mercy,
and on it goes, thousands of deaths or more
e time has no heart, no hearing
e leaves to where there is no healing,
venture in and leave no more,
the blood clots in the burning sands,
e evening flowers crowd in despair,
o suddenly at heart leave,
as, for it was not her,
e gone is forgotten,
e present is forgotten,
morrow remembers forever
leaf dances in the movement of the playful wind,
drop motionless when it pleases . . . .

ROBERT VARGAS

Blame It on the Reds

I

Thursday . . . crying . . . St. Peter's church . . . organ
Incense . . . lagrimas . . . 10:30 morning . . . sun/hot
Faces . . . old/young . . . Vincent gone
Anger/love . . . Chente gone now
Eunuch chronicles plastered with lies
Reds, Reds melting in American minds
Brought to you in living color by CBS
Dial soap and the puppet-coroners
of the TV world . . .
("Reds will make you dead," they squeal)
And the priest lites another candle/

II

Tears (saladas) . . . dry lips
Black hearse yawns/swallows
18 years of Chente . . . gone
Not killed in Cambodia . . . but war
(Padre nuestro que esta en los . . .)
Walking now . . . the last 24th st.
Business as usual . . . slower
Hundreds of sisters/brothers
Following behind/in you

---

lagrimas: tears
Chente (gone now): probably
    chente means people here
saladas: salty ones
Padre nuestro que esta en los . . .:
    our father who art in . . .

gered in love walking
st walls of cornucopia
lid-lined by Pig-nalgas
p signs gleaming
ars . . . Bank of America
d Glory still . . . stop/go
dre/Hija/Esposa . . . crying
antos . . . stop/go
ente en el medio de mayo
ne!
d the priest raises the chalice
This is my body This is my blood.")

III

uth Van Ness red light
cars now pollution (F-310)
restone Rent-a-Limousine stop/go
e mechanical centipede slowed
Progress stop/go
    Business as usual
ijo, hijo . . . te an asesinado!"
ust tapped him across the . . .

---

g-nalgas: pig-buttocks
dre/Hija/Esposa: mother,
  daughter, wife
antos: floods of tears, weeping
ente en el medio de mayo:
  people in the middle of May
jo, hijo . . . te an asesinado!:
  Son, son . . . they murdered you!

It seems an overdose of
business as usual . . . stop/go

IV

Look back
Look back Chente . . . si Puedes
Remember the Roach Pad hunger
Joys . . . highs, sorrows?
Mission sidewalks (BART raped)
Him goodbye pa siempre carnal
But the genocide trail begins su fin
Trembling with the weight of our guns . . . /
Chente 18 brown and dead
In the land of E Pluribus Unum
Dead in the land of the Apollos 13/
Edsel . . . Titanic . . . U2 and Gary Powers
Mission Hi . . . State College
                    and business as usual/

V

Now passing local draft board
Vision of monsoon flies
bloodsmell cheeks of bronze
Organisms shell pierced screams of death
Vietnam! Vietnam!
            Chente dies everywhere
            (Blame the reds!)

---

si Puedes: if you can
goodbye pa siempre carnal:
    goodbye forever, brother
su fin: its end

Cambodia . . . brown and 18 . . . Laos
  Chente dead in babylon
    (Blame the reds!)
En los barrios de Guatemala
San Francisco o Mississippi
      (Blame the reds!)

      VI

Holy Cross . . . silent in wait
Lagrimas de madre soak black lace
  Hijo. Hijo no te vayas
  Wife wails ripped/soul fright
      alone now . . .
Chente flows into open wound
In earth . . . magic dance of
Mayan ancestors . . . tears
Silent war drums sound
Chente killed by The Guardians
      of Enterprise
Then red white and blue
Phallic symbols thrust deep
    in our throats . . .
Moist dirt falls . . . covers
Ashes to ashes . . . peace brother
Peace . . . business as usual
    "Blame It on Reds!"

En los barrios de Guatemala:
  in the barrios of Guatemala
Lagrimas de madre: tears of a mother
Hijo. Hijo no te vayas: Son.
  Son, don't go.

Eskimo
Poems

Introduction

MADELYN SHULMAN

Eighty centuries past, the first Eskimo hunters followed the giant whale and the walrus across the steppingstone islands we call Big and Little Diomede. Their descendants range over the northern lands of half the world. Men of the ice fields, they call themselves "Innupiat," Men Preeminent, the original men whom the earth itself bore forth.

Their people live in lands that other men call Siberia, Alaska, Canada and Greenland. United by languages, cultures and a history of struggle in a region which yields no favors to its inhabitants, they are divided by lines of politics imposed by men who live to the south.

The songs and poems of the Innupiat reflect the land of midnight summer sun and winter darkness which gave them birth. They hold the optimism and courage of a people who found laughter on the brink of famine. Everyday songs passed the time during the tasks of the household. The hunter's songs reflect the fear, excitement, exultation of the pursuit of game or the lingering dread which struck as the sun receded each fall for its long journey to the south.

Songs reflect the beauty of the bursting-with-life summer arctic, multicolored by wildflowers and moist with the melted snows which the permanently frozen ice just a few feet down keeps close to the surface.

Bursting forth from the many emotions of a life in tune with nature, Eskimo poetry filled a need as great as food and warmth.

"For it is just as necessary for me to sing as it is to breathe," an Eskimo hunter told Danish ethnologist Knud Rasmussen in 1923. "My song is my breath," continued the shaman Orpingalik of the Netailingmiut Eskimo.

"Songs," he added, "are thoughts, sung out with the breath when people are moved by great forces and ordinary speech no longer suffices."

The men the arctic bred were hunters. They were tied to the animals they sought, as they were tied to each nook and cranny of the winter-shrouded tundra they called home. The hunter faced the familiar cold with equanimity; he feared the "unlucky hunt," the lack of game, the strange and fatal weather which could cause famine and death among his people. His life trembled on the brink of starvation, yet it was raised and supported to great peaks by the excitement of the hunt and the swift adrenalin rush of triumph at the kill. An inland Eskimo poet sang:

> A wonderful occupation
> Hunting caribou
> But all too rarely we
> Excel at it
> So that we stand
> Like a high flame
> Over the plain.

So the songs sing. They sing of the "bubbling food in the pot," the "hard, dearth times" of winter, the hundred myriad joys of living—joyous life even though death may be around a corner or the horrors of starvation and cannibalism only a winter past.

Sung in exultation and mourning, the poetry of the People forms part of a great and detailed oral tradition. There is no native Eskimo written language. Canadian Eskimo syllabic is the creation of a nineteenth-century missionary. The poetry which men like Rasmussen recorded during their journeys to the arctic two generations past stands as a monument to a tradition which today is dying in its clash with technological culture. Of the tens of thousands of Eskimo poets (the word "poet" in Eskimo means "to feel emotion") who did not meet a Rasmussen, we hear only echoes. Their songs, which in Eskimo tradition "belong to their owners," died with them.

The Eskimo people will survive. With the present generation tangled in the social ills of culture shock, a new breed of young Eskimo is emerging. Educated in white men's schools on Dick and Jane, American History and a million details of life in cities and on farms thousands of miles distant, a few young Eskimos are trying to bridge two cultures and live both —often at great personal cost.

"I can only know what is in my heart and spirit, and in the

ar reaches of my mind," writes Joseph Senungetuk of his ncestry. While his tradition ties him to the hunt, he can see hat way of life dying around him. In many villages only the ld people remember the language and legends—prey of anhropologists with tape recorders to preserve a few shreds. oday's hunter uses a snowmobile, rifle and motorboat, and if unting is "unlucky" he buys canned goods at the village tore.

"It was a hard life," writes Fred Bruemmer, who lived with he Canadian Camp Eskimos, "but it possessed the harmony nd balance that comes when men are free within themelves, secure within their society, and imbued with a feeling f kinship with all nature."

Glorious was life
Now I am filled with joy
For every time a dawn
Makes white the sky of night
For every time the sun goes up
Over the heavens.

Fairbanks, Alaska, September 1972

JOHN ANGAIAK

My Native Land, the Beautiful

... There is a windsong that chants
   a song
From past, present and future;
That chants from chill
   to morning cold.
"Come share our land, the beautiful,
Because you find as good no
   more."

NALUNGIAQ

Heaven and Hell

And when we die at last
we really know very little about what happens then.
But people who dream
have often seen the dead appear to them
just as they were in life.
Therefore we believe life does not end here on earth.

We have heard of three places where men go after
        death:
There is the Land of the Sky, a good place
where there is no sorrow and fear.
There have been wise men who went there
and came back to tell us about it:
They saw people playing ball, happy people
who did nothing but laugh and amuse themselves.
What we see from down here in the form of stars
are the lighted windows of the villages of the dead
in the Land of the Sky.

Then there are other worlds of the dead
        underground:
Way down deep is a place just like here
except on earth you starve
and down there they live in plenty.
The caribou graze in great herds
and there are endless plains
with juicy berries that are nice to eat.
Down there too, everything
is happiness and fun for the dead.

But there is another place, the Land of the Miserable,

right under the surface of the earth we walk on.
There go all the lazy men who were poor hunters,
and all women who refused to be tattooed,
not caring to suffer a little to become beautiful.
They had no life in them when they lived
so now after death they must squat on their haunches
with hanging heads, bad-tempered and silent,
and live in hunger and idleness
because they wasted their lives.
Only when a butterfly comes flying by
do they lift their heads
(as young birds open pink mouths uselessly after a
        gnat)
and when they snap at it, a puff of dust
comes out of their dry throats.

—English version by Edward Field
from the translation by Knud Rasmussen

CLARENCE PICKERNALL

This Is My Land

This is my land
From the time of the first moon
Till the time of the last sun
It was given to my people.
Wha-neh Wha-neh, the great giver
    of life,
Made me out of the earth of this
    land.
He said, "You are the land, and
    the land is you."
I take good care of this land,
For I am part of it.
I take good care of the animals,

For they are my brothers and
    sisters.
I take care of the streams and
    rivers,
For they clean my land.
I honor Ocean as my father,
For he gives me food and a
    means to travel.
Ocean knows everything, for he
    is everywhere.
Ocean is wise, for he is old.
Listen to Ocean, for he speaks
    wisdom.
He sees much and knows more.
He says, "Take care of my sister,
    Earth,
She is young, and has little
    wisdom, but much kindness.
When she smiles, it is
    springtime.
Scar not her beauty, for she is
    beautiful beyond all things.
Her face looks eternally upward
    to the beauty of sky and
    stars,
Where once she lived with her
    father, Sky."
I am forever grateful for this
    beautiful and bountiful earth.
God gave it to me.
This is my land.

SAMIK

Hunger

You, stranger, who only see us happy and free of
    care,
If you knew the horrors we often have to live through
you would understand our love of eating and singing
    and dancing.
There is not one among us
who hasn't lived through a winter of bad hunting
when many people starved to death.
We are never surprised to hear
that someone has died of starvation—we are used to
    it.
And they are not to blame: sickness comes,
or bad weather ruins hunting,
as when a blizzard of snow hides the breathing holes.

I once saw a wise old man hang himself
because he was starving to death
and preferred to die in his own way.
But before he died he filled his mouth with seal
    bones,
for that way he was sure to get plenty of meat
in the land of the dead.

Once during the winter famine
a woman gave birth to a child
while people lay round about her dying of hunger.
What could the baby want with life here on earth?
And how could it live when its mother herself
was dried up with starvation?
So she strangled it and let it freeze.
And later on ate it to keep alive—

Then a seal was caught and the famine was over,
so the mother survived.
But from that time on she was paralysed
because she had eaten part of herself.

That is what can happen to people.
We have gone through it ourselves
and know what one may come to, so we do not judge
    them.
And how would anyone who has eaten his fill and is
    well
be able to understand the madness of hunger?
We only know that we all want so much to live!

—English version by Edward Field
from the translation by Knud Rasmussen

TUKTU

Children of Nunamiut

He came out of the wind
    to sit by our fire,
    this man of the land,
    Nunamiut.
He had no pain;
    his words were sad.
He had lost his children
    taken by alien man,
    men from the sun,
    Tannik.
With his back to the high sun
    he sits
    silent now.
For thus they went
    to the high sun.

Following the sound of the juke
    box and new voices,
Nunamiut's children are gone
    with Tannik.
What is a man
    without children?
He is Nunamiut,
    and he too will be gone.
The land will be empty
    of man.
Gone the laughter
    across the snow.
Nevermore Nunamiut.
Soon there will be
    only the wind to cry
    for the children
    who are gone.
Listen, children, to the wind.
It speaks your father's tongue,
    the voice you would not use.
Remember your father
    was Nunamiut.
Only he could live
    with the wind.
Listen, Tannik, to the wind.
    What do you hear?
    What have you done?
Forever across the frozen land
    The wind will cry
    for the children of Nunamiut
    who are gone.

Igjugarjuk's Song

when I ran over the white fields
I met the great Musk Ox black
its hair shining for
the first time
grazing on flowers
far from the hill where I stood
I was stupid to think
they were small and thin
they grew up out of the earth
when I got closer
huge black giants
far from our houses
in the fields of happy summer hunting
I thought of shooting them

—*Reexpressed by Stephen Berg*
from Knud Rasmussen's Across Arctic America

ANONYMOUS

Eskimo Songs

I.

I'm asking because I haven't done anything
I'm asking the instrument for
$$help$$
$$she's\ a\ woman$$
because I haven't done anything to the people
they're looking
I can do anything
$$stabbing\ it$$
$$I'm$$
able to make it well

2.

If it wasn't a song
he wouldn't begin it
$$it\ was$$
this beginner
if it wasn't a song
it wouldn't be mine

3.

Knife
the people
instruments for partners
a man who is strong
the stick I dry stockings on

what's being skinned
                    what is big
                                    what is strong

       4.

My lamp
he walks around in the way
what are they going to do?
                                chew the skin of bootsoles
                                    to soften them
soft skin
I wish it would get soft quickly

       5.

Name of a man name of a man
who kills bear
                    the spearhole
here I am trying to drink blood
he pushed him down by the head
                                and the front of his
                                    inner coat
                                and the back of his
                                    inner coat

then girl
she isn't sorry
man who sleeps with her

6.

I'm crying I'm able to eat
I'm working well
                    when she desires
her husband or when he isn't angry
he comes off
it is enough he has another one
but not big it is enough he is old it is right
snow snow hoop of seal skin mouth spear
knife knife teeth mouth clothes
                                    a woman's hip
                                    muscles

7.

My mother in Padli
                    in the beyond
I am born my mother
because I'm in fat
                    because she deserves thanks
it is breaking
                    his neck
                        he chews it

8.

The man does he have land
                        another one?
it may be so
he wants me to sleep outside
I'm sleeping I'm getting up early in the morning
as soon as he comes

                        he is
giving me whiskey
Thanks.
the man
            let him have land
                         let's get going
it will be three of us
able to depart
                 his one time wife
will you kiss me?
                 She gives it
                 he's shivering
                 I won't keep still

9.

It's a dog Yes! I'm looking at him
he's snarling
                 get it quickly from below
                              I can see it
yet his ears
he has hanging ears!

10.

Let the man turn to me
this is a woman's song
                  probably
                         he's sleeping outside
I'm trying to stop freezing
he's getting up early
thanks

let the man turn to me
let him turn let you and I go
but your animals
                    your one time wife
they are leaving
                    she is pregnant

      II.

These
        the spirits because it is water
                                    if I
open it what is it?
It's this I swallow it because I don't wish to be
        laughed at
because I steer a straight course
his ass scratching it because it's bleeding
is it still bleeding?
are they skinned birds' tails?

      12.

And his kayak
he's looking at something big
name of man do you think I am dark
                                    and his kayak
name of man thank you thank you
my big wife
            I follow her around
                            only one
it's a five dog team
a little behind us

tiny bird
       I used to catch it

   13.

ut there his front I touch it
hat which is nothing
his We
ut there we are going to the ice
                           we ate bone
                           I'm not full
sweep the floor the cooking stove the possessions
      outside
e's piling more on the sled
kill a square flippered seal
                    the cooking place
call loud
' I divide it it is enough the
ossessions outside
            is that it?

   14.

ive it to me name of the baby
ome deer fat
        they are coming
ome deer marrow
         they are coming
nly his big mouth
his one fat from the stomach of the animal
                   frozen land
       now it's cold weather now he is shiny

I'm near the camp I'll warm you shall I carry it
he's showing me
                  sound
Wonderful!

     15.

Ursa Minor Ursa Minor where are they going?
where are they going?
not long until it is light not long until daylight
he troubles the dawn
he goes up to my house to my own house
I'm in my house
              here two people not long ago
they have been away babytalk babytalk
the lake has many turds
birdshit wet ones
            he is climbing on the hills
the elbow bone the blubber don't you see it?
                        No!

I see it why aren't you inside them
put your sleeves on put on your cap
have a big belly like a dead seal floating
rotten rotten
        the hole
(a Blackhead Island Eskimo here with me today)

     16.

wallpaper covers the tent the small tent
alive sounding
my knife a woman
speaking
       my knife a man speaking

e beaded front of a woman's only jacket
unding

ey hunt the square flipper seal and the whale
t quite night and lonely and his daughter
any young inhabitants of a place called

>   he is eating
>   me
>   his sleeping
>   boy
>   he's an old
>   man

is not afraid we are afraid
e young woman because she sleeps slept with a
    man

17.

unding
e cuts it
w he wishes
would like to fill her
>   now
have nothing to do
can't feel anything
e hooks it
>   in his hole
w
unding
>   now
    I have nothing to do

—English version by Stephen Berg Collected by Franz Boas

ANONYMOUS

Men's Impotence

Perhaps—well
It may not matter!
Perhaps—well.
I sing merely of him,
"the boiling one,"
Who sat, fearful, his mouth fast closed,
Among women.

Perhaps—well
It may not matter!
Perhaps—well.
I sing merely of him,
"caribou stomach,"
Who sat, fearful, his mouth fast closed,
Among women.
His two eyes ill-boding
Bent like a horn
To be cut into fish-spears!

Perhaps—well
It may not matter!
Perhaps—well.
I sing merely of him,
"the axe,"
Who sat, fearful, his mouth fast closed,
Far, far away from man,
In solitude.

Perhaps—well
It may not matter!

Perhaps—well.
My tongue merely joins words
Into a little song
A little mouth,
Curling downwards at the corners,
Like a bent twig
For a kayak rib.

—English version by Edmund Carpenter

ANONYMOUS

Who Comes?

Who comes?
Is it the house of death approaching?
Away!
Or I will harness you to my team.

—English version by Edmund Carpenter

ANONYMOUS

The Dead Hunter Speaks
Through the Voice of a Shaman

To be beyond you now, to feel
joy burning inside me when the sun
burns thru the terrible sky
To feel joy in the new sun, aie!
in the sky's curved belly

But restless more likely, restless
These flies swarm around me, dropping
eggs in the rotting collarbone,
into my eyes, their cold mouths moving
I choke on such horrors

& remembering the last fear, I remember
a dark rim of ocean, remembering
the last fear, the broken boat drifting,
drawing me into that darkness, aie!
Now the other side holds me

& I remember men's fear in the boats
I see the snow forced into my door, fear's
shadow over the hut, while my body
hung in the air, the door hidden, aie!
When I cried in fear of the snow

Horror stuck in my throat, the hut
walled me in, slowly the ice-floe broke

rror choked me, the thin sky
vered with sound, the voice
the dark ice cracking, cold mornings

—English version by Jerome Rothenberg

ONYMOUS

e Song of Kuk-Ook, The Bad Boy

is is the song of Kuk-Ook, the bad boy,
  Imakayah—hayah,
  Imakayah—hah—hayah.
m going to run away from home, hayah,
a great big boat, hayah,
  hunt for a sweet little girl, hayah:
hall get her some beads, hayah:
e kind that look like boiled ones, hayah:
en, after a while, hayah,
hall come back home, hayah,
hall call all my relations together, hayah,
d shall give them all a good thrashing, hayah,
hall marry two girls at once, hayah,
e of the sweet little darlings, hayah,
hall dress in spotted sealskins, hayah, and the other
lear little pet, hayah,
all wear skins of the hooded seal only, hayah.

—English version by Heinrich Rink

ANONYMOUS

**Dead Man's Song Dreamed
by One Who Is Alive**

I'm so happy
when it's dawn
up over the sky,
I'm so happy
when the sun crawls
up over the sky.

Without this
I'd be so scared I couldn't eat,
I'd see maggots
eat their way in
at the bottom of my collarbone
and in my eyes.

Here I am, remembering
how choked with fear I was
when they buried me
in a snow hut out on the lake.

When the last block of snow
was pushed in I couldn't see
how my soul could fly
to the land of hunting.

The doorblock worried me
and I shit
when the fresh-water ice split in the cold
and the frost-crack grew, thundering
up over the sky.

Life was a glory
in winter
but did it make me happy?
No! I was always anxious
to get seal-skins and kamik skins.

I'm so happy now
every time dawn
stains the night sky white,
every time the sun rolls up
over the heavens.

—English version by Stephen Berg

ANONYMOUS

In What Shape?

In what shape
Shall I wait at the breathing-hole?
In the skin of a fox
Will I wait at the breathing-hole!
In the skin of "the leaper"
Will I wait at the breathing-hole!
In the form of a wolf
Will I wait at the breathing-hole!
What do I want at the breathing-hole?
To catch seals!

—English version by Knud Rasmussen

ANONYMOUS

a woman's song about men

first I lowered my head
and for a start I stared at the ground
for a second I couldn't say anything
but now that they're gone
I raise my head I look straight ahead I can answer
They say I stole a man
the husband of one of my aunts
they say I took him for a husband of my own
lies
fairy tales
slander
It was him, he
lay down next to me
But they're men
which is why they lie
that's the reason
and it's my hard luck

—English version by Armand Schwerner

ANONYMOUS

the old man's song, about his wife

husband and wife we loved each other then
we do now
there was a time
each found the other
beautiful

but a few days ago maybe yesterday
she saw in the black lake water
a sickening face
a wracked old woman face
wrinkled full of spots

I saw it she says
that shape in the water
the spirit of the water
wrinkled and spotted

and who'd seen that face before
wrinkled, full of spots?
wasn't it me
and isn't it me now
when I look at you?

—English version by Armand Schwerner

ANONYMOUS

spring fjord

I was out in my kayak
I was out at sea in it
I was paddling
very gently in the fjord Ammassivik
there was ice in the water
and on the water a petrel
turned his head this way that way
didn't see me paddling
Suddenly nothing but his tail
then nothing
He plunged but not for me:
huge head upon the water
great hairy seal
giant head with giant eyes, moustache
all shining and dripping
and the seal came gently toward me
Why didn't I harpoon him?
was I sorry for him?
was it the day, the spring day, the seal
playing in the sun
like me?

—English version by Armand Schwerner

ANONYMOUS

the choice

while she was berrying
she bore that child
laid it on grass
and berried some more
she came back, creeping

she came back, creeping
and sprang forward
screaming
to terrify that child
then she left

she came back, creeping
and did those things again
once twice three times
the fourth time the child
changed it was a bird
flew away

—English version by Armand Schwerner

ANONYMOUS

dream

I dreamt about you last night
you were walking on the pebbles of the beach
with me
I dreamt about you
as if I had awakened
I followed you
beautiful
as a young seal
I wanted you like a hunter
lusting after a very young seal
who plunges in, feeling pursued.
That's how it was
for me.

—English version by Armand Schwerner

ANONYMOUS

Utahania's Impeachment*

Something was whispered
Of man and wife
Who could not agree.
And what was it all about?
A wife who in rightful anger
Tore her husband's furs across,
Took their canoe
And rowed away with her son.
Ay—ay, all who listen,
What do you think of him,
Poor sort of man?
Is he to be envied,
Who is great in his anger
But faint in strength,
Blubbering helplessly
Properly chastised?
Though it was he who foolishly proud
Started the quarrel with stupid words.

—English version by Knud Rasmussen

* Utahania impeached one Kanaijuaq, who had quarreled with his wife and attempted to desert her, leaving her to her fate out in the wilds; the woman, however, had proved not only able to stand up for herself in a rough-and-tumble, but left her husband of her own accord and went to shift for herself, taking her son with her.

ANONYMOUS

spider

alone
in the sky
she and her son

great hunter
he killed
reindeer
they kept the sinew
for a long rope

alone
in the sky
she sewed him up
in a skin
alone
in the sky

she let him down
the sinew rope
he became a spider

—English version by Armand Schwerner

ANONYMOUS

Travel Song

Leaving the white bear behind in his realm of sea-ice
we set off for our winter hunting grounds on the
      inland bays.
This is the route we took:
First we made our way across dangerous Dead-man's
      Gulch
and then crossed High-in-the-sky Mountain.
Circling Crooked Lake
we followed the course of the river over the flatlands
      beyond
where the sleds sank in deep snow up the cross slats.
It was sweaty work, I tell you,
helping the dogs.

You think I even had a small fish
or a piece of musk-ox meat to chew on?
Don't make me laugh: I didn't have a shred on me.
The journey went on and on.
It was exhausting, pushing the sled along the lakes
around one island and over another,
mushing, mushing.
When we passed the island called Big Pot
we spit at it
just to do something different for a change.

Then after Stony Island
we crossed over Water Sound at the narrows,
touching on the two islands like crooked eyes
that we call naturally, Cross-Eyed Islands,
and arrived at Seal Bay, where we camped,

and settled down to a winter season
of hunting at the breathing holes
for the delicious small blubber beasts.

Such is our life,
the life of hunters
migrating with the season.

—*English version by Edward Field
from the translation by Knud Rasmussen*

ANONYMOUS

song of the old woman

all these heads these ears these eyes
around me
how long will ears hear me?
and those eyes how long
will they look at me?
when these ears won't hear me any more
when these eyes turn aside from my eyes
I'll eat no more raw liver with fat
and those eyes won't see me any more
and my hair my hair will have disappeared

—*English version by Armand Schwerner*

Hawaiian
Poems

Introduction: The Hawaiian Oral Tradition

Hawaii (formerly the Sandwich Islands) was annexed by the United States in 1898 and became a state in 1959. About fifteen percent of the 650,000 population is partly Polynesian, while fewer than one thousand are pure-blooded Polynesians.

The California poet Michael Nicholas, who studied in Hawaii, says that as far as contemporary poetry goes Hawaii is just like any other state. But among the fifty states Hawaii does have a cultural background that is unique: a vigorous oral tradition of song, poetry, folk tales and stories that dates back hundreds of years. This material was not collected and written down until the nineteenth century. Today it is virtually unknown except to specialists in the field. With two exceptions, our Hawaiian selections have been taken from this ancient material.

The following brief account of the ancient poetry was given in a lecture by Mrs. Kzwaka Pukui, outstanding authority on Hawaiian literature:

"Hawaiians were lovers of poetry and keen observers of nature. Every phase of nature was noted, and expressions of love and observation were woven into poems of praise, of satire, of resentment, and of celebration for any occasion that might arise. These poems, or *meles,* were not recited but chanted.

"There are many interesting characteristics of Hawaiian poetry. Hula poems had lines of uniform length, but the *oli* poems vary considerably in length in different parts of the poem. This unevenness did not destroy the rhythm or the smoothness of the flow, because there never was any attempt at rhyming at the ends of lines. King Kalakaus was the only Hawaiian to attempt a poem with rhyming words.

"The poets of old Hawaii were skilled in the use of words. Carelessness in the choice of words was believed to result in death for the composer or the person for whom it was composed. Words and word combinations were studied to see whether they were suspicious or not; and in that there were always two things to consider, the literal meaning and the *kaona* or inner meaning. The literal meaning is like the body and the *kaona* is like the spirit of the poem.

"The poets of old Hawaii were skilled prosodists. Many poems did not hold to one thought alone. Two lines might be about a ship, the next two about a bird on a tree. Such sudden and apparently fickle changes in thought might sound peculiar or jerky to a European, but to a Hawaiian it was perfectly comprehensible because the *kaona* told the consecutive story. Persons were sometimes referred to as rains, winds, ferns, and so on. A person might be referred to in the same poem as rain in one piece and as a flower in another.

"The *kaona* of a chant was believed to be potent enough to bring lovers together, to mend broken homes, or break up an undesirable union. But it was ineffective unless chanted before a gathering of people, and so the composer looked for such an opportunity. Birthday celebrations were especially liked for the debut of a poem. *Meles* were composed for almost every and any occasion and for every emotion—love, hatred, jealousy, admiration, or woe.

"From birth to death *meles* were composed for the *alii* or nobility. When a visitor came, *meles* were composed; if his leis or garlands were beautiful, they were sung about; if he were fond of surfing, that was a theme for a *mele*; and if he liked to travel by canoe, that, too, was sung about.

"Chants 'belonged' to the person or family of the person to whom they were dedicated or for whom they had been composed. Others were not allowed to use them except to repeat them in honor of the owner. In order to preserve chants, however, it was necessary to take some old chants belonging to a person long dead and revise and rededicate them to living persons in the family.

"There were different styles of chanting, called the *oli*, the *kepakepa*, the *hoaeao*, and others.

"The *oli* was used for prayers, prophecies, dirges, and chants not intended for dancing. The melodies consisted only of two or three notes, and were usually chanted in a monotone. Occasionally there was a slight change of pitch. The *kepakepa* differs from the *oli* in the prolonging of the end of each line. It is a form much used in love chants. The *mele hula* or *hula* chants were used for dancing and ranged over several notes, in contrast to the chanting in other *meles*. The old Hawaiian music was more rhythmic than melodious."

A. Grove Day writes about "The Kumulipo," from which we have selected several passages:

"It is a sacred creation chant and a genealogy of one of the great *alii* families, traced from the beginning of the world. An authentic primitive poem of more than two thousand lines, it was carried in memory from one generation of court reciters to another.

"Pagan though they were by Christian standards, the Hawaiian Polynesians were as powerful and godly a people as ever existed, constantly in touch with divine beings. But instead of venerating one omniscient god, they worshiped four principal deities and countless minor ones. There was a different god for every phase of activity, for every form of life, for every individual. The gods populated the earth, the sky, the sea, the underground—fish gods, household gods, gods of war and gods of sports, of planting and harvest, of hula dancing, and tapa beating, of vegetation and volcanoes, of major gods, less important gods, and demigods, with galaxies of hobgoblins, guardian angels, ghouls and ogres to fill all gaps in the natural and supernatural world.

"Hawaiian reckoning went only to 400,000, so the priests acknowledged allegiance to 400,000 gods, but that was an underestimate, for there were many more gods than people, and no god-fearing individual would undertake any action of consequence without first consulting some divinity.

"In the 1860's, before this idolatry had entirely passed from memory, Abraham Fornander (1812–1887), a Swede who had settled in Hawaii in 1842, began to make a collection of ancient Hawaiian tales. His marriage to an island princess and his employment in a number of government positions, including a circuit judgeship on Maui, gave him trusted access to all levels of society. With the assistance of several respected Hawaiians, who did most of the actual collecting and recording, over a period of twenty years he assembled a mass of manuscript which was eventually published as *The Fornander Collection of Hawaiian Antiquities and Folklore.*"

Our selections are taken from this collection.

WALTER LOWENFELS

Dirge*

I make this dirge for you Miss Mary Binning I miss
    you
o my daughter the wind of Na'alehu used to scatter
    the dust in our house
o my daughter at the Lau-hu cliff
I'm crying for missing you and let it be; I love you I
    see us
o my daughter at the cold Ka-puna spring our water,
    in the rain
that the Ha'ao hill undergoes
up the trail almost nobody knew, us alone o my
    daughter
I'm missing you my life turns
a shade grayer forever
it's over now, you on your road endlessly who use to
    shine so my darling,
now in the one direction, away, me still in these
    places,
on a walk, up a hill, next to the spring dampening
    me, bent
from this stone yearning
                o precious
as pearls, in Waikapuna the sun warmed you I didn't
    know you
from the flowers

---

* Composed by Mrs. Mary K. Pukui's mother after the death of her
infant. Reexpressed by Armand Schwerner.

LARRY KIMURA

For Ha'Alo'U

call to the woman moving in the fog
the fog of Pu'u'ohu creeping quietly down onto
    La'ela'e
the sacred hill of the chiefs of Waimea
serene are the upper parts of Hoku'ula
the higher regions of Kilauea lie spread out
Pu'u Kapu remains in calmness
sacred is this hill until the single birth in the
    blood-red rain
red, red is the water of Waimea
like blood vessels flowing down
from the uplands of Kohokohau and Haumea
some Spanish blood has the wandering lady
in the Kipu'upu'u rain nipping sharply the skin
of the woman for whom is the chiefly land
    Koaka'iniki
Koali'ula is for the last resident of Naihe'auhau
swim in the waters of Wai'auia
at Waiaka the meeting with the waters of 'A'ali'i
reach the rise of Lauhuluali'i
at Ahuli, turn and come back with a wreath
an adornment of young palai fern in the reddish
    tinged hair
Vapors of mist wisp gently from above Ouli
the rainbow appears for you woman
Answer oh beloved guardian of the royal secret cave
Love with the delicate overflowing water of Waihaka
The water spreading over the cherished land
filling the heart to the brim
Answer oh one who bends over the sovereign
    acknowledging sea of Kahiki

The Water of Kane

I want to know
where the water of Kane is.
Tell me, is it at
the eastern gate
where the sun floats up,
at Haehae?
Yes, that's where it is.

Is it in clouds resting
on the skin of the ocean,
in the mountains,
the valleys,
under heavy rains,
in mist,
in the holy cloud of the Gods stained black?
Where is it?
I want to know, tell me if it's
in the deep springs of earth,
in the magic powerful water
of life,
in clouds shaped like everything on earth,
on the huge breast of the ocean.
Is it?
Yes, that's where it is.

You have to tell me!
Life! O Give us this life!

*—English version by Stephen Berg
from the translation by N. B. Emerso*

The Kumulipo*

At a time when the earth became hot
At the time when the heavens turned about
At the time when the sun was darkened
To cause the moon to shine
The time of the rise of the Pleiades,
The slime, this was the source of the earth
The source of the night that made night
The intense darkness, the deep darkness
Darkness of the sun, darkness of the night
    Nothing but night.

    The night gave birth
    Born was Kumulipo in the night, a male
    Born was Po'ele in the night, a female
    Born was the coral polyp, born was the coral,
        came forth
    Born was the grub that digs and heaps up the
        earth, came forth
    Born was his child an earthworm, came forth

---

* *Kumulipo* is a sacred creation chant and a genealogy of one of the great *Alii* families, traced from the beginning of the world. An authentic primitive poem of more than two thousand lines, it was carried in memory by one generation of court reciters to another.

Our selection comprises the opening stanzas and a refrain. It is from a modern translation, with an analytical commentary by Martha Warren Beckwith. As read literally, it "seems to picture the rising of the land out of the fathomless depths of the ocean. Along its shores the lower forms of life begin to gather, and these are arranged as births from parent to child." Like most Hawaiian poetry, however, it has meanings hidden in symbolic language; and essentially "it is a birth chant, and procreation is its theme."—A. Grove Day

Born was the starfish, his child the small starfish
    came forth
Born was the sea cucumber, his child the small
    sea cucumber came forth
Born was the sea urchin, the sea urchin tribe
Born was the short-spiked sea urchin, came forth
Born was the smooth sea urchin, his child the
    long-spiked came forth
Born was the ring-shaped sea urchin, his child
    the thin-spiked came forth
Born was the barnacle, his child the pearl oyster
    came forth
Born was the mother-of-pearl, his child the oyster
    came forth
Born was the mussel, his child the hermit crab
    came forth
Born was the big limpet, his child the small
    limpet came forth
Born was the cowry, his child the small cowry
    came forth
Born was the naka shellfish, the rock oyster his
    child came forth
Born was the drupa shellfish, his child the bitter
    white shellfish came forth
Born was the conch shell, his child the small
    conch shell came forth
Born was the nerita shellfish, the sand-burrowing
    shellfish his child came forth
Born was the fresh-water shellfish, his child the
    small fresh-water shellfish came forth
Born was man for the narrow stream, the woman
    for the broad stream
Born was the ekaha moss living in the sea
Guarded by the ekahakaha fern living on land
Darkness slips into light
Earth and water are the food of the plant

The god enters, man cannot enter
Man for the narrow stream, woman for the broad
    stream
Born was the tough sea-grass living in the sea
Guarded by the tough land-grass living on land
  . . .

REFRAIN

Man for the narrow stream, woman for the broad
    stream
Born was the hairy seaweed living in the sea
Guarded by the hairy pandanus vine living on land
Darkness slips into light
Earth and water are the food of the plant
The god enters, the man cannot enter

The man with the water gourd, he is a god
Water that causes the withered vine to flourish
Causes the plant top to develop freely
Multiplying in the passing time
The long night slips along
Fruitful, very fruitful
Spreading here, spreading there
Spreading this way, spreading that way
Propping up earth, holding up the sky
The time passes, this night of Kumulipo
    Still it is night

—English version by Martha Warren Beckwith

The Night-Digger
[*from* The Kumulipo]

The time arrives for Po-kanokano
To increase the progeny of Po-lalo-uli
Dark is the skin of the new generation
Black is the skin of the beloved Po-lalo-uli
Who sleeps as a wife to the Night-digger
The beaked nose that digs the earth is erected
Let it dig at the land, increase it, heap it up
Walling it up at the back
Walling it up in front
The pig child is born
Lodges inland in the bush.
Cultivates the water taro patches of Lo'iloa
Tenfold is the increase of the island
Tenfold the increase of the land
The land where the Night-digger dwelt
Long is the line of his ancestry
The ancient line of the pig of chief blood
The pig of highest rank born in the time
The time when the Night-digger lived
And slept with Po-lalo-uli
The night gave birth
Born were the peaked-heads, they were clumsy ones
Born were the flat-heads, they were braggarts
Born were the angular-heads, they were esteemed
Born were the fair-haired, they were strangers
Born were the blonds, their skin was white
Born were those with retreating foreheads, they were
    bushy-haired
Born were the blunt-heads, their heads were round
Born were the dark-heads, they were dark

Born were the common class, they were unsettled
Born were the working class, they were workers
Born were the favorites, they were courted
Born were the slave class, and wild was their nature
Born were the cropped-haired, they were the picked
    men
Born were the song chanters, they were indolent
Born were the big bellies, big eaters were they
Born were the timid ones, bashful were they
Born were the messengers, they were sent here and
    there
Born were the slothful, they were lazy
Born were the stingy, they were sour
Born were the puny, they were feeble ones
Born were the thickset, they were stalwart
Born were the broad-chested, broad was their badge
    in battle
Born were the family men, they were home lovers
Born were the mixed breeds, they had no fixed line of
    descent
Born were the lousy-headed, they were lice infested
Born were the war leaders, men followed after them
Born were the high chiefs, they were ruddy
Born were the stragglers, they were dispersed
Scattered here and there
The children of Lo'iloa multiplied
The virgin land sprang into bloom
The gourd of desire was loosened
With desire to extend the family line
To carry on the fruit of Oma's descents,
The generations from the Night-digger
In that period of the past
    Still it is night

—*English version by Martha Warren Beckwith*

from a chant to Kualii

no comparison, no comparison
                    impossible
o could I say no I could not say you're like
the crooked naio, bastard sandalwood
or the thick garland of the motherless ahihi flower
white-fringed in Nuuanu
you're not the deep pool trodden by swimmers, not
the fine, the silvergray leafed hinahina, silver-sword,
        bending
to lean and then to fall
in the wind
No, Ku, you're not like any of these
or maybe like the great ohia forest woods
these islands' lehua forest wood alone in the ninth
remoteness of the jungle
No, Ku, these are not like you
not the ekaha fern, strange whole-leafed that lies
under my bed-mat for warmth, not
the fragrant ekaha, not the changing olapa leaf
which gives us a blue dye, the olapa bark,
which gives us a blue dye
No, Ku, you're not like any of these
not the rain, kehau, great
vessel of water poured out, bringing
morning land breeze, not the cold Kumomoku
mountain breeze, the cold Leleiwe land breeze
haven't you known, do you know
the mountain breezes that double up your back
that make you sit crooked and cramped at Kaimohala
No, Ku, you're not like any of these, not

the fragrant lipoa sea weed lovely tasting
not the red fresh-water crab
within the pond
upon the top
    of Mt. Kaala, not
like the kukui trees of Lihue
whose rough bark the sun splits
as the Awa-root liquor cracks our skin
you're not like any of these, Ku
not like the fine aalii tree whose leaves cure us
not the maile tree who gives us twinings
both glossy and fragrant
for our happy times together, not like the kokio
whose solitary flowers drop wilted, not
like these, you're not like any of these Ku,
      not porpoise
of the sea-cutting snout at home in the shark's water
or the oo, Kaiona bird, ablaze
with yellow shock of feathers; or the keen pig,
the chief-searcher, who sniffed out Umi the king
for the holy Kaoleoku egged on
by the rainbow dazzling him to his wonder;
haven't you known, do you know
that woman on Puukapolei's summit, draped
in her yellow cloth, draped in the brilliance
crushed from the mao tree flowers, you're not
like the wiliwili wood whose seeds
compose our bracelets, whose trunk glides, whose
    body
lithe among the breakers is surf-rider
you're not even like the tree called ti, the great
giver, its leaves around our baking supper, leaves
to carry it out, healing leaves on the pounding
brow, leaf cool for the fevered head, gift of the leaf

laced in the fishing-net, necklace of the leaves
dispelling bad spirits, and gift of the dizzying
okolehau liquor from its sweet baked root O Ku
you're not even like the tree called ti.

—*English version by Armand Schwerner*

Lamentation for Lahainaluna*

Love to you Lahainaluna,
We are the orphans longing to be with you . . .
You are the kawelu (grass) at
     the cliff of Nuuanu;
At Nuuanu, the dividing line of
   knowledge,
Seeking for you but never finding you.
There you are at the Isthmus of Darien,
Overlooking the Mediterranean Sea.
O Lahainaluna, I love you.
You are the sounding twine of the
   shoemaker;
You are the sledge hammer of the
   blacksmith;
You are the compass of the navigators;
And the mud-hen singing at midnight.
I heard a noise while asleep and awoke,
O Lahainaluna, I love you.
You were a hunchback among the chiefs;
You were the consulting companion of the
     two winds,
The moae and the haupepee.

* From certain of her students when they heard they were to leave the
Seminary of Lahainaluna because the building was decaying.

They are the originators of the kona,
To hide away your love
Across to the stormy sea of Cape Horn.
O Lahainaluna, I love you;
Thou art the misty rain of Lilikoi
That is agitating my heart.
You have seen Waialeale,
You were delighted with the water
      of Haunu,
    Lovely Kaala sublime in its beauty,
It was the beauty of the land,
You are the fragrant flower of Ainahau,
        that is kissed in all lands.
In the midst of people, and the jungle of
      Africa.
I love the lehua blooming on the plain,
Satisfied in the sojourn that was blessed
      by the red rain,
Murmuring at Kauehoa.
You were a friend in time of trouble at
      Lahainaluna,
Just like the pervading of perfumes
Flying over to the calm of Lele.
I jumped to embrace you, but could not
      find you
You were at Ieheulani.
Beautiful lies the field of Kaiwiula.
O Lahainaluna, I love you.
The greatest in the Kingdom of
      Hawaii nei.

—English version by Abraham Fornander

the woman who married a caterpillar

Kumuhea the night-caterpillar loves the woman
with his daylight man-body takes her for wife,
    handsome
man huge caterpillar, at night
gorges on sweet-potato leaves
Kumuhea huge night-caterpillar
bloated back home mornings
soft Kumuhea flabby Kumuhea, through
him shiftless the wife starves
Where does he go nights, her father says, Where
does he go nights, says the hemp string
his wife fastens to track him where he goes nights;
after him through brush on his crawl
the long string snarls, the night-
caterpillar is strong with anger, tears
into leaves all around
    the people cry Kane help us
    night-caterpillar kills our food, do him in
    in his hill-cave home, he
    kills our food
merciful Kane slices him to bits
we now call cut-worm cut-worm cut-worm

*—English version by Armand Schwerner
Collected by Mary K. Pukui*

Taunt Song
A warrior replies to his daughter who has asked him to teach her husband a certain stroke with the war-club.

my club-stroke's for me not him,
                    sandpiper
mincing along the beach, hello wave
goodby husband
                    banana-tree trunk
stalwart on a calm day, hello south wind
goodby husband
who's the stroke fit for it's fit for your father
who really occupies space from crown
to toenail
                    in the south wind
he stands
                    he also makes it
fronting the north wind
                    when *he* fails
he takes the clumped root-earth with him

—*English version by Armand Schwerner*

Puerto Ricans in the U.S.A.

Introduction
DAVID HERNÁNDEZ

We are thought of as quiet, friendly, simple happy people. We do not riot, go on strike, nor are we studied by agencies and schools and novelists as much as our fellow humanos. Not yet. The blancos visit our island, take pictures of natives with happy white teeth in brown skins and the new Burger King and Kentucky-Fried Chicken franchises. The blancos come back after vacation to show their movies and slides to their friends. Three or four blocks away live the city Puerto Ricans. The blancos think that we have melted into the American-Dream/Rags-to-Riches society, that we have disappeared in the cities. Blanco, I will show you a movie in the everyday life of a Rican that came to Los Estados Unidos/U.S.A. I will show you the American Dream in practice:

1. DREAM: I come down the mountain
            mud in my feet,
        the trees rustle gently
            and the sun is warm
            and I sit outside the store
        where the old men meet
            and I drink Malta Corona
            and think of Los Estados.
        Someday I will leave here
            and life will be better,
        I will not be angry or sad
                like my friends who write their
                letters.

2. CHICAGO: When I was little and brown,
            the sound of the plane stopped.
                Midway Field was there
                proud of my white shirt
                blue shorts

white shoes
blue socks.
True Puerto Rican proud.
Excited by the americans
              and their smiles like the
                   coca-cola
              ads nailed to the town's
                   walls.
And I was confused and shivered
when the Chicago /December wind
                   hit me.
I was little and brown.

3. DREAM: En Los Estados our son will be a great
              man.
CHICAGO: And he grew up with filth
              and hate for cops and teachers and
                   welfare
              and the priest who came for lent-money
              but was never there when he cried.
              little by little
                   he died.
              through school he lost his hope and
                   dropped out late.

4. DREAM: Our daughter will be a happy and
              dignified senorita.
CHICAGO: While they talk of violence,
              you just don't feel right.
                   hustling your body
                        to the businessman,
                   showing you his wallet-pictures
              of 2 children, a home, a car and a wife.
              yesterday your neighbor's baby
                   got killed playing with a
                        knife.

5. DREAM: Everything we've dreamed about will
              come true.
CHICAGO: Look at junkie man!
                   peeking one way then the
                        other.

stealing from his own
mother.
Junkie man!
I am an old man of twenty-eight,
sitting here on these steps,
eating here on these steps,
candy-bars, potato-chips,
pepsi, wine,
waiting here for my fix
of dreams, subtle colors,
remembering to breathe when my lungs
go slow
fastly, before the needle is out of my
vein.

6. DREAM: We will have the best of food and plenty
of milk.
CHICAGO: Gotta cop some wine.
no money, no
food-stamps,
not even 20%-alcohol Listerine to drink,
ha! that's a laugh jack,
but it isn't so funny.
knees are weak,
ears hear screaming ambulance,
windows shutting,
the pain of someone
being cut
the anger of someone cutting.
some wine jack,
a taste of wine

7. DREAM: En Los Estados there are good jobs and
beautiful houses.
CHICAGO: He goes to work
in a factory
every hot and cold day,
making money for a
two-room
pink and blue
apartment

with urine-stenched
stairs,
and roaches for house
guests,
and the virgin mary with extended rosy
hands
to bless the home.

8. DREAM: We will be known and respected.
CHICAGO: WHY DO YOU WANT WELFARE?
I am going lame and in the
factory these three fingers
were cut off.

DO YOU HAVE CHILDREN?   2.
ARE THEY IN SCHOOL?   no.
WE WILL CONTINUE TOMORROW SINCE IT IS
MY LUNCH HOUR.
I KNOW IT IS YOUR 4TH DAY HERE, BUT YOU
DID NOT LISTEN
FOR YOUR NUMBER!
My name is Don Carlos
Angel Valdez.

9. DREAM: Everyone is equal en Los Estados.
CHICAGO: Winter.
The tans are gone.
MINE STAYS.
Two dollars and twenty-eight cents at the
drug-store
makes one brown.   Me?
I have been
paying
since my
arrival.

10. DREAM: We will settle in a neighborhood with
good stores, good schools,
good hospitals and big tall churches.
CHICAGO: You come/We go.
We pack our rice and beans,
our Goodwill furniture

and nelson brothers t.v. set.
we pack nando's, nino's, and varella's
    grocery stores.
we pack arroyo's liquor store.
we pack our sons and daughters and
    their special school books
for socially-mal-adjusted children.
we pack our gang-boppers with hearts
    and wooden faces
and their gym shoes and purple shirts
    that they wore in "West-Side
Story" singing "i just met a girl named
    Maria,"
but maria's in the hospital getting her
    tubes tied
after a miscarriage.
we pack our bolitas/numbers man.
we pack our flies and politician
    promises.
we pack our store-front pentecostal
    church.
we pack halsted street and the landlord
    notices telling us to leave
to make room for buicks and hip
    volkswagens.
       to move out as our shouts fall on
           ears that sympathize
       but offer to help us pack.
       to move again where no one will
           hear
                     feel
              taste or smell us
like doña ruperta at lynn brothers
    funeral parlor.
we pack like the first time we came here
    by plane.

You hold in your hands el corazon y alma/heart and soul of my people. Our poetry. Read what my Rican sisters and brothers have written.

no one knows me,
i am thin like puerto rican air on the mountains.
i walk down the street
and see my people waiting.
all with wooden faces and boiling-lava feelings in
side.
no one knows me.

Do you still think we should be quiet and friendly and
colorful? The volcano is erupting.

AIME CARRERO

Neo-Rican Jetliner

Ticket please
> Me recuerda ese señor
>> a Dick Tracy
>> a Trucutú
>>> (Alleyoop *en inglés*)
> Ahí viene otra vez
> con el 'no se ponga de pié
>> por favor'

Fasten your seat belt

> Ahí viene esa señorita
> con el 'abróchese el cinturón
> en seguidita please'

> please' por favor
>> plis
>> plis

No smoking *señor*
> Is this seat taken?
> No. Please.
> Thank you.

This man reminds me of Dick Tracy, of Trucutu (Alleyoop in
  English)
Here he comes again
with "Don't stand up, please"

Here comes this young lady
with "fasten the belt
right away please"

Are you from over here?
No Sir from New York
But you look Puerto Rican.
I'm not I'm not born in New York
     born in New York

No smoking please
 My name is Raúl.
 From Puerto Rico?
 Jes an'now from Noo Jork.
 Muee bieeen senhor
 Raúl is may name *señor*.
 American— you look American
     blond
    you don't look Puerto Rican:
 Raúl *señor* my name is Raúl.
 R-A-U-L u.u.u.
 Like the U you find in fool?
 Jes. U.U.U. fool.

Fasten your seat belt fasten your seat
Fasten your fasten fast fast fast
F-f-f-f-s-s-s--t-t . . . .

   VUELO A

 New York the center of the world is big the
dream my father had when the sugar cane died
of drought Sir and bad fertilizing Sir did its job
to force his wings open to search for the greatest
money on earth the dream my father had.

Vuelo: flight

CONVERSACIÓN I

Hey boy
Le tengo miedo a esa voz.
  'We the people of the United States
  in order to form
  Hey boy
  I am scared of that voice with the
  Hey boy
  'a more perfect union,
  Hey boy
  'establish justice,
Me duele esa voz con el
  Hey boy
Me duele esa voz como un SUR
  Hey boy
  'insure domestic tranquility
Me duele el color de esa voz
  con
  el
  Hey boy
  and so on
  and so on
  promote the general welfare,
  Hey boy it is it
  and so on

CONVERSATION I

Le tengo miedo a esa voz: I'm afraid
  of that voice
Me duele esa voz con el: I'm hurt by that voice with the
como un SUR: like a south wind
el color de esa voz: the false sound of that voice

and so on
'over the land of the free
Me duele, me duele esa voz. . .

. . . .

Hey boy did you see
        did you see

VUELO B

New York Sir the center of the world gave
birth to my little kid sister yeah and you know
the doctor said and the nurse said when the
other doctor and the other nurse showed up with
my kid sister Sir that no other baby was as big Sir
as my kid sister Sir was.

CONVERSACIÓN II

My friend is big man
a new man man Neo-Rican
a big man man
Big man, my friend is big
Neo-Rican
A Jetliner man
As big as I can say big car
big as fire man
As big as I can say mountain
    as I can say sky
    my friend is big
    big man big
    as the dry season
    as the rain
    big as I say
    my friend is big
    big man big

As big as I can say Manhattan
    my friend is bigger
    the size of God
    The Jetliner
    Neo-Rican
    MAN . . .

VUELO C

New York the center of the world taught me
law-stick ball pool the street money man—the
wings my father saw but forgot to take when he
saw them there man everywhere anyway in the
law in the street in the money.

CONVERSACIÓN III
La primera vez que la escuché
    en mi primer viaje
    me sonó poética
        esa frase
        o gráfica
    algo así

CONVERSATION III
The first time that I listened to it
on my first voyage
it sounded poetic to me
that sentence
or like a drawing
something like this

S.O.B.
Yes Raol like *CERVEZA*
     the word to me
     is a girl
Oh Raol you're nuts

. . . .

Man you spelled his name bad

. . . .

How?
     R-A-U-L like fool
Jes like foool

Ah Raool sounds like fool
a U like fool

Jes fool U like foool
U U U   fool

VUELO D

New York the center of the world taught me
law yes Sir the color of the wings my father
found when he came to forget his land yes Sir
and decided the wings money can buy were bet-
ter than the land.

CONVERSACIÓN IV

A ver mi hermana he venido
Hace tiempo no la veo

Cerveza: beer

CONVERSATION IV
I came to see my sister,
I haven't seen her for quite some time.

Slow please did you say NANA
  No señora hermana dije hermana
    Sister *dije* sister
  That I come to see her
     you see?
  La pobre no se levanta
Is she sick?
  Si señora.
Is she old?
  yes yes *no se puede mover*
I am sorry to hear that.
  podía caminar
  la última vez que la vi
Is she sick?
  yes yes

Is she old?
  yes yes
I'm sorry to hear that

No, madam, sister, I said sister.

The poor woman can't get up.

Yes, ma'm.

She can't move.

She could walk
the last time I saw her.

LAMENTO 3

This Puerto Rican is silent
This Puerto Rican is sad to be silent and sad
I feel something big
          or low
          or dark
          is going on
          in the back
          of the mind man.
This Puerto Rican is silent and sad.
The color no white man dares to ask.

LAMENTO 2

I was born in New York new blood.
I was born in New York
I'm not a Jones Act Puerto Rican.
yeah?
I'm a Neo-Rican man   new flash.
yeah?
I known what I know no Jones Act man
yeah?

. . . . . .

what was that   ?

LAMENTO I

Hay horas de espalda: sin terminar
Jetliner warned—you're high

LAMENT I

There are times (hours) which turn their back on you: endlessly

Hay horas de frente: ahí puestas, tranquilas
Jetliner cracks
Hay horas de día: que hay que caminar
Overshoot—too high
Hay horas de hombre: volar
cracks open
Hay horas . . .
CRASH   in the dark

LAMENTO O

On the fringe of trouble if you ask
        ¿ por qué señor
            por qué?
On the fringe of trouble I say
        ¿olvida el Jones Act?
On the fringe of trouble I say.
        a chance sir do we have
        a chance sir a chance?
We cannot solve your problems I say
On the fringe of trouble again
On the fringe   . . .

There are times (hours) which face you: put here, quiet

There are hours of the daytime: we have to walk

There are hours for man: fly

There are hours . . .

por qué: why   *¿olvida . . . ?:* are you forgetting?

VICTOR HERNANDEZ CRUZ

Afterword

poems are songs. poems cry & laugh.
a poet is in the world/the world is in the poet.things
are in the world.rock is hard/you better believe me
slam a rock against your face.you see.
where they come from is where the poet was/the
      poet
was there/or the poem grew out of mind/but the
      mind of
the poet is there.
EXPERIENCE
poets records his life/his love of life.
his woman is a poem/& what they do together can if
      the
poet wants be poetry or it's poetry all the time.
words are what the poet uses/he bounces words to
sing his feelings.
in the world the poet goes thru fire & ice.

thru ugly ugly cuts/or beautiful dreams.
burning yellow bodies is part of present american
      every-
day life.
dead indians on t.v. is common.

these are respectable things (situations or perfect
      happenings
there are poets of these respectable things, they write
poems about it, how they like to kill people.
kill being a good four letter word.

poets go in & out of worlds/people are in the world.

met a woman on 72nd street & she is fine.
or saw a picture of dead people.
or the Paxton Brothers put swords thru indian
        woman
with their babies in their arms.

the poet sees&hears the world.& there are many
        worlds.

people live in different worlds (got different bags)
humans talk/dance & make noise/a poet must make
        poetry out
of that/or make poetry out of his mind/which took
        form from
the world.
words & music travel.
god would not make anything bad or dirty.some
        people
make dirty things happen tho.

i see what's in the world & sing it
like god.

JOSÉ-ANGEL FIGUEROA

a conversation w/coca cola

i speak now/coca cola
        the way a stone is born
    of your tongue of raw meat
        and teeth like tombstone

you roam east side streets
        where corner lights speak spanish everyday
    and like picasso/you
        want to become the sole dictionary
    of el barrio's feet/don't you

don't you know
        that bodegas feed negritos
    and picante makes the food feel good
        so that your alka-seltzer communions
    won't be necessary to digest
        that yellow latino grease
    which makes rice pegao
        the only confirmation
    and constitution of our land

don't you know
        that new york jibaros
    will never give in to herman badil lo's
        dixie peach & plus white toothpaste
            philosophy

---

negritos: black boys   *pegao:* sticky
picante: hot peppers   *jibaros:* peasants

and that jibaritas will never carry
    their hopes in high heels
to become deaf & dumb to the true meaning
    of their existence
in exchange for miss clairol's push-down spray
    and dead traditions
of does she or doesn't she miss subway realities

i speak now/ coca cola
    the way a stone IS born
for the plaster that came crawling down
    from the tired blemished ceiling from above
that loses its vision when night invades
    the voiceless will of day/woke me up!

woke me up/coca cola
    and told me that the only life
which made sense anymore are those graves
    that can't speak english
and which are kept from crying
    like pigeons sleeping in the rain

and told me/coca cola
    that the only sense
which made life anymore are those restless
    streets
    that get ulcers everyday
knowing boriqueños are held in dying tension
    ever since ajax nixon
sent that white knight to clean spik & span's
    mind
    from knowing that the red stains

---

jibaritas: peasant women   *boriqueños:* Puerto Rricans

        of the sweat and pain of his brown flesh
            was nothing but the ketch-up
        mr heinz left behind before he made you/coca
            cola
                the king of latino's brow

    and told me/coca cola
            that latino souls wake up
        like swollen dreams in the middle of the night
            ever since con edison
        raised the rent & the landlords executed the hot
            water
                that was to come back from retirement
        before the month's rent made itself welcomed
            to molested mail boxes
        who couldn't speak spanish or spell latino names
            correctly unless he's called
        tito or chico or mr. spik
            the one with the welfare tribe upstairs

    i speak now/coca cola
            knowing that you have suffocated
        the only air left from my flowery-carpeted room
            & that your roaming thru latino streets
        has caused perverted corridors/street alleys
            and tar-smelling roofs to become
        the final playground and cemetery where el
            barrio
                gets babies born with Death Buttons
        pinned to their Life Day nipples
            while parked cars have funeral processions
        for those that get hit by brute winds and
            cold drunken nights every morningday night

    but now/coca cola
            i speak the way blood vessels break

and the way saliva can turn to fire
    for the aging paint of my cracked walls
revealed my sleepless eyes the truth:
    to know that latinos have
for too long been succumbed to the religious
      diarrhea
    of walter cronkite liberals
who wrote the yellow pages of wooden verses of
      liberty
    and nursery rhythm jack and jill
went-up-the-hill jive to handcuff jibaro's mind

but now/coca cola
    i can see like the corner lights
that speak spanish everyday
    and realize why snoopy
was always nodding and took his ass to the moon
    for he knew that unemployment agencies
which were now opening on sundays
    would never stop tropical sons
from crying out in the middle of the night:

    mami! mami! tengo hambre!
    tennnngggoooo o hambre!

    I'M HUNGRY!
bellyaching every morning to the next
    from an overdose of suffering

for he knew/coca cola
    why barretto kept slapping his mad conga
while crying out: de donde vengo?/de donde
      vengo?

---

de donde vengo?: where do I come from?

when you made latinos suffer
from lack of sun & homemade mama/papa skin.
love
and rice & beans which made them men
and baptized their morning naturalness

ah! but his message touched
the ear drums of my mind
and told me/coca cola

that la justicia
is not a yearly xmas gift

DAVID HERNÁNDEZ

Señora Medelez

señora medelez chicana
of
azteca bones and blood
in
your woman body that was/is beautiful
hard is your
face from times that were/are
bad
and you señora medelez know what hunger is
and your children also know
they are older now and you loved
and cried for them
that is why

---

la justicia: justice

your
    face is hard.
and where is joe your oldest son?
      married after a year
    in jail
        so now he's gone and you've
        got 5 left after lucy at 15
got pregnant
       married came back and
               her husband is
               in jail at 19.
      señora medelez
your eyes are cold and small
your mouth set unmovable like the time you went to
the station for hitting a cop
      you said nobody hits my children.
          nobody!
  the pyramids of aztecas
             still are proud
and tall with sands of the desert in
            the wind
and sun as
    the cactus grows wild

the things
    left are strong as the aztecas and
        señora medelez the
      pyramids are beautiful
     like you
    when asleep
        in the city.

JESUS LEDESMA, JR.

Chicago Is a Hell of a Place

In this city
you are a man at ten.
You learn to hate.
You learn to steal,
cheat lie and run mighty fast.
Cause someone's always after you.
In your own block
it is your world for tea, or maybe some L.S.D.
Go ask at the corner,
it's like a discount store
if you know what I mean.
Chicago is a hell of a place,
full of anger and hate,
the smell of Puerto Rican rum, sweet smell of tea
coming out of a gangway
wino sleeping in an alley.
Pimps singing $5 dollars
for a piece of my bitch!
gangsters walking down the street,
saying don't get in my way
or I'll stomp you.
Hear the police siren and say in your mind,
who is it this time?
See a dog shitting on your stairs
See the wino pissing at your door
See the pimp pimping his bitch
See the pusher hustle his stuff
See the junkie copping his stuff.
Come and see Chicago,
        It's a hell of a place.

JOSÉ LLUBIEN

City Poem V

Some one wrote a poem
About a Puerto Rican family
Every summer they would all
Eight of them crowd a window
to the street and city magic

Soft eyes with purple flame
Red fire burns/pupilas
flame of spanish/moorish Karma/African (flame)
Damnation in hell
on a hummer Puerto Rican faces
were seen down under in the garment district
Hombres bad Hombres todos
Leeching some crumbs off Americano nothingness
Motherfucking Immigrantes all with a lot of heart
All machos
who stole/fought/killed/died dead
And pinched and fucked virgin white Americanas
Our skin/our language/our looks latinos
O beautiful for spacious mountains majesty
says Animals!
O josé can you see
from the dawn's early light
you are an . . .
Yes
an Animal!
without heart

---

pupilas: pupils of the eyes   *todos:* all of them

So in anger we animals
Chew gillette razor blades
and spit red spic blood
it runs heavy and deep to the ground
without mercy we write our testimony on subway
    trains

We frighten white Americanos and yell at fat
    heartless Policías
Hate burns the deepest
when it is cursed with Blood
Ours we cannot swallow/ we spit out
our hate runs/wheels and deals on subway tracks
    forever
America we find the beautiful is Ugly
it has no heart/no corazón.

In our jungle without trees
we ride heavy with our lost dreams
we shoot dope/eat dope/watch dope grow
within/ one cold dark dying moment
frozen in the white veil of deadness
eased from fear/ numbed from hunger
Resting forever without installment plans
That now our beaten bodies rest
weary Puerto Rican bones
And Fulano-Mengano invites
To celebrate the parting of many lives
Bembe tonight !
Bembe tonight !
for the dead respect laughter and music
For we the living loved them all.

Policías: policemen

Heart/ we got big mucho corazón
We feel the pain and listen to the music
heavy with beat/ beats of life to come

Drum beat heaviest
Temba tin
tumba tin tan
Rumba tan tin
bam bam ba
cumbamba
That our spirits drive away loneliness
misery that reminds us every day

FELIPE LUCIANO

Spies going to the cooker

Spies going to the cooker
never realizing they've
been cooked
Mind shook, money took
And nothing to show for it
but raw scars, railroad tracks
on swollen arms
And abcesses of the mind

Go ahead spic
Stick it in your trigger finger
You ain't got nothing to lose
but your freedom
And yo' mama—who wails futilely at
the toilet door
wants to tear down the whole plumbing structure
but can't

cause you still inside
Shooting up, when you already been shot

You ain't got nothing to lose but your freedom
Shoot the poison, the smack of your oppressor
Shoot Pepi, on 8th Ave. pulling a mule cart
of cheap dresses
to be sold en la Marqueta

Shoot Mami, sweating like her brown ancestors
long ago, killed by Columbus and the Church,
to make that 6o.oo in the tombs called factories
Machines rape your mother everyday and spit her out
a whore—
Don't throw dagger stares at men
who cruelly crunch your
sister's buttocks between
slimy fingers

You ain't doing nothing
to change it spic
You ain't got nothing to lose
but your freedom

Shoot up our island
of Borinquen
Populated by writhing snakes
who we nicely call gringos
Green Go
Green Go

Green Berets en el Yunqua
Green Marines on Calle del Sol
Green bills passing from trembling hand
to callused palms,

And you shoot the poison 'cause you don't
want to stare at your own ugly reflection—

But it's there spic, hanging off the stoops,
dripping over on firescapes, in the eyes
of your hermanito, who wants to be
like you—when he grows up.

Better get hip—Quit lying and jiving
and flying like you own something
Cause you don't own nothing but your chains
And when the revolution comes
Very, very soon—You shoot, and I'll shoot
You shoot and I'll shoot, You shoot and I'll shoot—

And unless you shoot straight
I'm gonna get you
Before you get yourself!

CARMEN MARTINEZ

ugliness #5

> i heard her talking:
> 'man, if i had a rainbow . . .

shyly deafness tickled at my head
> i use to kneel too
> > and pray with faith
> and then wait . . .
> wait to wake up

---

hermanito: little brother

wait for the train
wait for wednesday
            or him
            or a chance
but mainly for a change
and sometimes . . . just once in a while
i'd even wait for
                    tomorrow
            or a poem
            or simply my next breath
usually, though i'd wait
            for what was underneath
            to commit my special crime
            to be able to scream LOUD
but now, i merely wait
            to fall asleep and forget/

    and she continued:
u know what else i/d do with a rainbow . . .

JULIO ARCÁNGEL MARZÁN

An American Dream

(for Jose De Diego*)

I entered the hall where the family of my history
Waited. They stood to greet me. Offering his hand,
Charles the Fifth praised me for coming, at his
        command,
The gathering was seated. Distant members, each a
        mystery,

* The late Nationalist poet, famous for his dedication to Puerto
Rican Independence.

Introduced themselves. *Rodrigo de Vivar. El Savio.*
　　Then,
Formalities done, he led me to a room behind a
　　curtain
Where, gowned in the red of a great lady, Mother
　　Spain
Sat poised, waiting. With her voice, her lyrical blend
Of East and West, she urged me forward. Warm, her
　　small,
Mother's hands, delicately strong, held mine. When
　　she asked
If I would leave again, she wept and quickly masked
Her tears behind a fan. Charles had returned to the
　　hall
Where the family danced to a guitar. She heard them
　　clap,
And then she knew. I smiled and laid my head upon
　　her lap.

PEDRO PIETRI

Broken English Dream

We got off
The two engine airplane
At idlewild airport
renamed kennedy airport
Twenty years later:
with all our furniture
and personal belongings
in our back pockets

We followed the sign
that said welcome to america
But keep your hands off

the property, follow the green
Arrogant arrow to confusion
don't walk don't talk don't think
Just drink and we will not sentence you to rot in
        prison

So this is America
land of the free for everyone
but our family
So this is america
where you wake
up in the morning
to brush your teeth
with the home relief
the leading toothpaste
operation bootstrap
promised you you will get
everytime you buy
a box of cornflakes on the lay-away plan
So this is america
land of the free
to watch the
adventures of superman
on tv if you know
somebody who owns a set
that works properly
So this is america
discovered by columbus
in fourteen ninety two
with captain video
and lady bird johnson
the first miss subways
in the new testament
So this is america
where they keep you
busy singing

en mi casa toman bustelo
en mi casa toman bustelo

To the united states we came
To learn how to misspell our name
To lose the definition of pride
To have misfortune on our side
To live where rats and roaches roam
And sing a house is not a home
To be trained to turn on television sets
To dream about jobs you will never get
To fill out welfare applications
To graduate from school without an education
To be drafted distorted and destroyed
To work fulltime and still be unemployed
To wait for income tax returns
And stay drunk and lose concern
For the heart and soul of our race
And the weather that produces our face

To pledge allegiance
To the flag
of the United states
Of installment plans
One nation
Under discrimination
For which it stands
And which it falls
With poverty injustice
And air conditioned
Firing squads
For everyone who has

---

en mi casa toman bustelo: in our house we drink Bustelo coffee

The sun on the side
Of their complexion

Lapiz: Pencil
Pluma: Pen
Cocina: Kitchen
Gallina: Hen

Everyone who learns this
Will receive a high school equivalency diploma
A life time supply of employment agencies
A different bill collector for every day of the week
The right to vote for the executioner of your choice
And two hamburgers for thirty five cents in times
    square

PIRI THOMAS

A First Night in El Sing Sing Prison

I stand on the hill, on top of the rocks,
I stand and I look and stare inside,
And remember, the whole, the mass, the past. . . .
I see the gray figures, like walking alone,
The blast of the then, the walking alive,
I look and remember. . . .
      I was there with you once. . . .

I was with you, I search into the building,
Many years ago break through the walls,
I see my cell block, my cell, my bunk, my wash bowl,
    my ca-ca bowl,
I see my grim bars, around and around,
The long march upward to the dining room mess.

I do not see them playing, I hear only the marching,

The long line, upward climb, a gray . . . a sea gray,
A mass of thousands of identities, thousands of locks,
   thousands of keys.
Look, I cry, the cells are open—
Wake up . . . I can't, I'm not asleep, I'm dreaming,
   Piri.
Can you hear the clicks of thousands of keys being
   turned?
The soft pad-pad of the back, the man, the turn of
   your back so he'll not see your face.

The gripping of the wash bowl—the dizziness will
   pass
Sit on your bowl . . . crap . . . move your bowels. . . .
Defecate . . . oh, man, do something, don't just sit
   there.
Make them shadow bars go away,
Count the bolts on your cell, how big it is . . .
6 x 9 x 8 . . . who cares?
It could be Grand Central Station, it's too small for
   me.

Smoke a smoke, read a book, plug your ear
   phones . . .
Shut out, drown out, don't listen, don't hear, don't
   look,
Don't let it get to you.
Forget the green dark pressure that pulls you in a
   short while back.
Forget the last hard flung look before your back was
   trapped by a hard flung gate,
Forget your loss of clothes, identity, forget your bug
   killing shaves,
And the spread your cheek inspection, or lift your
   feet, puleese.
Forget the damp filled cell in the box, no room in
   reception.

Forget the two matches left in the book,
And three tailor-made smokes.
Forget your splitting these in half
And now four matches and still three tailor made
    smokes.

Forget laying on the dingy mattress . . . . . .
And inhaling time and no space.
Forget the damned filling, the hammering damned
    filling.
As—it roars on you. . . .
Hard—into your mind.
You drag your burning cigarette.
Oh God, here it comes.
Fifteen uptight years. . . . . .of this.
                Gee whiz. . . . . Hope I make it
                              Got to . .
                              Got to . .
                              Got to . .

JUAN VILLEGAS

WSLUM Presents
12 o'clock high or (How to get 15,000 feet off
the ground without really trying)

fly brother, fly
so high
    so so high
        a city high
            a rooftop emancipation high
fly brother, fly
        data-data-data-data-data.
      ALTITUDE: 400 rusty fire escapes . . . Roger.

BEARING: 2000 untouched garbage cans by 3000
definitely touched roaches . . . Roger.

VELOCITY: full speed of a 1972 oldsmobile, with
four wheel drive, air conditioning,
stereo component system, avocado
hood; and built in magnetic, auto-
matic pay toilet with reusable paper
. . . Roger.

WIND VELOCITY: cold as hell . . . Roger.

RADAR: no sign of the man . . . Roger.

PRESSURE: uptight, everything's a mother . . .
Roger for days.

fly brother, fly
and when the time comes to descend
to come
    down
       to
          earth,

    then it is
    when you shall go to meet
    the important one; el hombre,
    the man, the provider,
    the all knowing, the omnipotent,
    the image of your reflection, the
MAN FROM GLAD, MAN FROM GLAD,
oouuoouu, oouuooouuu!
    he is your sponsor, the producer
    of your plastic melodrama . . .
    aren't you glad you use dial,
    don't you wish *somebody* did?

fly brother, fly
so high
   so so high
      soar above the lights
      of Sodom brother
      fly brother, fly.

Related Poems by White and Black Americans

Introduction
CLARENCE MAJOR

What is the difference between the humming of an electric can opener and the humming of an insect in the grass on a hot summer day. What is the difference between the ringing of a telephone and the ringing of a cowbell. Tell me how the music from a turntable differs from the music of a flowing river. Show me the space between a slaveship and a relationship.

What does it mean, that first sound—*da*—we each make.

I do not know the names of the plants growing in various colorful pots in my red window here in Manhattan. I see them and *know* them beyond naming them. *I* could name them and that would probably reinforce what I see when I look at them. To name plants or animals or ideas or situations is to define the world. These plants have different personalities. I already recognize them by their personalities. By their needs. Some need more water than others. Some need more light than others. Some are deep green, others are light green. Some are tough, others are frail. Some can stand the cold of open windows in winter, others become ill. They are each different, even the ones that seem alike are very different.

What and who one *is* is a social thing that changes the shape of that original *da*. Different cultures, different needs. Yet all the same, so clearly the same. Understand the need to touch and to be touched. Not only the flesh.

Defining the world, it depends on the angle. The unique situation of North America and its many visions has left large spaces between these various visions. Chicanos, Blacks, Eskimos, Indians, Hawaiians, Jews, Puerto Ricans, Italians, Poles, Germans, English, Irish, Welsh, others. Yet there are ways to oversimplify everybody, everything, reduce people and ideas to what can be coerced or ignored or loved. You define the world you want to see. The world you do not want to deal with you define as inferior or nonexistent.

But the eye of the poet is open. His ear hears the thump of his culture, the pulse of his people; and once the skin is peeled away the throbbing arteries are recognized to be those of ev-

[231

erybody, regardless of how they have been previously defined. One has to see—see clearly the place where one is standing, where one moves. Understand who and what one touches.

Some of our North American poets have recognized themselves as part of all life and others have not. Some have seen and continue to see themselves as experts on life rather than part of it. Most white poets fall into this last category. Black American poets, for the most part, while using a language with a white personality, have used and still use their folk and musical roots as sources, beginning points.

I see those plants in the window. The central need is to define what one already knows. Claude Levi-Strauss says a myth, in the classical sense, is a story that aims to show *why* things are as they are. The white poet in North America who recognizes and uses values other than white values, in a sense borrows a Fire and takes it back to his people—in the mainstream. They call him a genius for his originality. The Black American poet who insists on being himself usually has no space, no world ready to accept him. The white or Black poet who knows the ring of a telephone may be able to define his own actions in society, but if he does not also understand the humming of an insect in the grass, there is a whole area of his own experience that remains closed off to him.

Yet for a poet to see and use the Fire of a culture other than his own is the oldest love story around, and since humanity has always felt itself on the brink of total disaster, its need for love stories—as many as possible—will go on forever!

April 4, 1972

ETEL ADNAN

The Battle of Angels

We threw into outer space
a whole maze of Indian tribes
with nuclear garbage
as unwanted satellites

the Omaha Indian sings:

Arise, sun, moon, stars, all of you
who move in the heavens
I pray you, hear me: in your midst
a new life has come.

His song is
drilling holes in our ears
hammering its way into the Mountain Speech of
        Memphis
our Revelation

The Black Prophet
ascended twice:
to meet the sun
and to meet his death

—remember the kites falling when we were children
they always looked like dying birds—

In the dark rooms of the
movie houses the films of Prophecy
contaminate the audiences. Batman
Gagarin Superman Martin Luther King
this is the Battle of Angels.

ROBERT BLY

Anarchists Fainting

You United States, frightened by dreams of
      Guatemala,
building houses with eight-mile-long wings to
      imprison the Cubans,
eating a bread made of the sound of sunken buffalo
      bones,
drinking water turned dark by the shadow of
      Negroes.
You remember things seen when you were still
      unable to speak—
white wings lying in a field.
And when you try to pass a bill,
long boards fly up, suddenly,
in Nevada,
in ghost towns.

You wave your insubstantial foot timidly in the damp
      air.
You long to return to the shell.
Even at the start Chicago was a place where the
      cobblestones
got up and flew around at night,
and anarchists fainted as they read the *Decline and
      Fall.*
The ground is soaked with water used to boil dogs.

Your sons dream they have been lost in kinky hair,
no one can find them,
neighbors walk shoulder to shoulder for three days.

And your sons are lost in the immense forest.
And the harsh deer drop,
the businessmen climb into their F-4's
the chocks are knocked out,
the F-4 shoots off the deck,
    trailing smoke,
dipping as if haunted by the center of the ocean,
then pulling up again, as Locke said it would

Our spirit is in the baseball rising into the light

So the crippled ships go out into the deep,
sexual orchids fly out to meet the rain,
    the singer sings from deep in his chest.
Memory stops,
    black threads string out in the wind,
the eyes of the nation go blind.

We look out the window, and the building across
        suddenly explodes.
Wild horses run through the long hair on the ground
        floor
Cripple Creek's survivors peer out from an upper
        story,
    blood pours from their ears,
the Sioux dead sleep all night in the rain troughs on
        the
    Treasury Building.

The moonlight crouches over the teenager's body
        thrown from the car
The weeping child like a fish thrown from a herring
        block

the black-nosed Avenger leaping off the deck

Women who hear the cry of small animals in their
      furs
and drive their cars at a hundred miles an hour into
      trees

MILLEN BRAND

Behold Beloved

Not only Count Zinzendorf
proselytized the Indians:
the Reverend George Michael Weiss, a "Reformed
      pastor,"
suggested to the Classis of Amsterdam
that churches be established
to "win the affections" of the Indians.
In Seventeen Thirty
the Reverend John Philip Boehm
wrote a letter saying that at Oley
Weiss "celebrated the Lord's Supper
without previous preparation"
and "baptized at the same time
a number of children, among whom
(as is reported) were also Indian children
who, as unbelievers,
go about like wild animals,
without a knowledge of God or His word."
The Reverend Weiss persisted
and in Seventeen Forty-two
sent painted pictures of the "wild men"
to Europe, pleading for them.
He said they were "very interesting."

He said he had talked with them
and had baptized many of them
"at their request." He expressed surprise
that "no sufficient urgency" was felt
"for the conversion of these savages."
The Classis next year wrote back
encouraging him
"to bring over that waste of wild heathendom."
But some said
the Reverend Weiss's baptisms
were "unscriptural actions."
In anger against "the principle of conversion,"
Boehm wrote, "Behold beloved . . .
where did our Lord command this?" As usual,
it was impossible to find in Scripture
what one did not want to find.
Indians "are imbued with blood
knuckle deep." They tear and devour
"even as the bear or other wild beasts do."
They are "wrapped up in the fog and misery
of their iniquity." One could obviously
do nothing for them and in that case,
many implied, it was best,
since they were in the way, to kill them.

OLGA CABRAL

General Custer Enters Hell

*". . . this is just like the Indian wars, except that the
    helicopter has replaced the horse."*

All the flags of hell flying
        General Custer enters hell
in good flying weather
        on an ICBM
                & wearing
all his medals of the
        Battle of Mississippi
                2 brassballs & a
                paper hat
tours hell accompanied by
        a pack of phobic moons
& inspects a think-tank
        where technicians are giving
                a prisoner of war
                the water-torture.

Who lies there is neither
        man nor woman any longer
                but a country
barefoot: the same
        brown/black feet of the
                shoeless poor
who have walked centuries down the
        Andes or along the Ganges
                everywhere in time's
                ghettos.
General Custer instantly

recognizes them from photographs
of Most Wanted Feet & is
rabid
to see they have caught the last
guerrilla of ages & now
pyromaniacs have set fire to
the prisoner's eyes & his country
will die with his brain.

Still hell is not secure. Somewhere
in a secret hideout under hell's vast
graveyards the
guerrilla of ages has returned
disguised as a newborn infant.

HAYDEN CARRUTH

At Dawn

At dawn the desert turns to porcelain.
Upon a dune-rim stands a skeletal horse,
Head down, forehoof cocked, cropping glazed sand.

The stars blanch like goldfish in a frozen pond.
A lizard darts from the F-hole of a violin
That lies in perfect syntax on the sand.

Sunrays set the horse on fire. Behind
A giant cactus a shy Indian screams
Century after century in his death pains.

WILLIAM CHILDRESS

For an Indian Woman Dead in Childbirth
[written at an archaeological site,
Dickson Mounds, Illinois]

Death stopped your
attempt at life, long
before Columbus came,
and took you from your
mud hut to lie in state
before these gawking
strangers. Fibers
of flesh still halo
the loins that grip
the tiny warrior
who would not leave you.
His thin ivory wrists
still grope toward
a life that never came.

I think of the shamans
whose witchcraft failed
to unclench your pelvis;
you could not give
what would not be given.
I watch the gaping
tourists who, with
Kodaks ready, picture
your pain; and, mother,
I am in pain and I
become your son,
centuries late
transcribing
your passing.

LEO CONNELLAN

This Is A Stick-Up

El Welfare Chevito slunk out of his urine stench Casa
to feed a needle to the fella sitting down on the nerve
      ends of his bowels
like some impaled Prime Minister slipping his feet
      on a greasy pole
where he can get up off and can't.

Evening just turned dark touched lovely people like
      you and me
with soft caressing breezes, but El Welfare Chevito,
      like a victim of croton oil.
Crave jabbed murder onto his relief screeching brain.
      Pastrami gorged Police
sitting on the wide buttocks of no exercise, waited to
      get their sex with
six guns.

And up the avenue innocent victim in the white
      apron of piety
that concealed the one eighthworth of Virginia ham
      he gave you after
you paid him for half a pound, made the slot man at
      the Daily Spread Eagle
his morning headlines for the big shots laying down
      cents for a copy
like it was nothing.

It was over in a minute, light flashed on light
throwing the good guy's glasses off his sneak thief's
      surprised eyes
stamped with a gasp muffled by his shoulders hitting
      groceries

falling all over him like stir crazy cons leaping
      hopelessly nowhere.

But outside, slinking up with their winking whores
      light
to kill forever the seed of a life, the wide blue
      bottoms
had El Welfare Chevito blasted into street with so
      many holes in him
it was hard to get in a last dream of far away Puerto
      Rico.

JEFFERSON DAVIS

John Mason Gets Sassacus' Head

John Mason dreams
at dusk, as fat flies buzz,
thump the glass pane.
Starved among summer feedings
John Mason shuts his eyes . . .

the bombers clock out
from Connecticutt west
stuffed with dark fiire
to char wild India
at last
John Mason dreams
"to destroy enemy
sanctuaries."

He wakes
the head is brought to him
eyes quenched
lips quieted with thongs

the head of Sassacus
and his hands
cut off lest they reach
into a dream's shadow
dark waves of blood
spilled to feed flies.
John Mason sleeps

and dreams again . . .
from his dull eye
empty locusts of iron
fall onto dark bodies
who glow and sow the earth
till their eyes are broken
by the iron teeth
and fire without light
eats their tongues

John Mason dreams
this is "pacification"—
he feels at
peace
gut furnaces
of Texaco crack blood
to gasoline
maggot ball bearings
rip and eat their flesh
wallow and grow wings
the bombers land
again and stalk to rest
John Mason dreams

he is safe, gorged
alone, asleep, burrowed

deep in his steel home
beyond all flies
eyes lights hands
tides of blood
and he dreams
what he has mastered.

DOUGLAS FLAHERTY

Snake Rite
[improvisation on the Zuni
Indian legend of New Mexico]

The blind beetle
calls for drink
We hunters watch
from the tall grass
rigid as spears
The Spider Woman
winks an evil wink
All the snakes
sleep in their rattles
Beyond the grass
water surrounds us

The dove sings
We cast off clothes
We stand naked
and ready to drink
with the snakes
Fully awake now
they slither
& suck our tongues

Like mother milk
it brings strength
This makes us glad

Now we drink the
fluid of spiders
Come come and drink
I ya oha e
The warriors
find their children
They crawl in the grass
Now we are ready
to bathe them
Come with reverence
Come all people

JOHN GILL

Something More Ghostly

This is not an unkind land
upstate New York
Finger Lakes Region
where glacial lakes keep their cold
til mid-July
and rocky canyons bring the water down
past great falls and cliffs of shale
to fill bony fingers:
Skaneateles, Owasco, Cayuga, Seneca, Canandaigua
ghostly names still treading the past
not used—"recreation areas," hopefully, on the map
where early bright empire cities
Elmira, Binghamton, Bath,
Geneva, Watkins Glen, Aurora, Auburn . . .

their Victorian grace and gimcrack gentility
linger in a faint smell of dust,
a few streets, or the way the light is sometimes laid
grey and nostalgic like the heartless past
of Empire and Sullivan's stolid march and rape
where even his men, their war-whoops of joy
less commanding, grew tired of destroying
such quantities abounding:
tons and acres of corn piled and burnt,
delightful peach and apple orchards girdled,
villages wiped out so the savages won't come back.
No adventure left, his raiders saw the land,
returned to divide and farm and speculate.
"Why, them Indians had fine log houses
windows filled with something looked like glass.
Better than what I had back East!"
So we came
where even now we camp on conquered ground
right off the highway
and something more ghostly rings us in
a restlessness, a vague fear, a distaste
as simple as the weather
for this quietly spectacular land
whose ancient people, Seneca, meant "people of
        stone."
The stones remain.

JOHN HAINES

The Traveler

I

Among the quiet people of the frost,
I remember an Eskimo
from Holy Cross, walking one evening
on the road to Fairbanks.

II

A lamp full of shadows burned
on the table before us;
the light came as though from far off
through the yellow skin of a tent.

III

Thousands of years passed.
People were camped on the bank
of a river, drying fish
in the sun. Women bent over
stretched hides, scraping
in a kind of furry patience.

There were long hunts through
the wet autumn grass,
meat piled high in caches—
a red memory against whiteness.

IV

We were away for a long time.
The footsteps of a man walking alone
on the frozen road from Asia
crunched in the darkness
and were gone.

WILLIAM HARMON

Adaptation of Nahuatl Lament

Ha: If I introduce you into the obscure bowels of the
          Temple
& ask which bones belong to the omnipotent
          Achalchiuhtlanextin,
     first chief of the ancient Toltecs,
Or of Necaxemitl, devoutest pontifex,
If I inquire as to the whereabouts of the peerless
          beauty of
     the celebrated empress Xiuhtzal,
Where nowadays the most pacific Topiltzin, last
          monarch of
     hapless Tulan,
Or the location of the sacred ashes of Xolotl our first
          father,
     or those of ring-giving Nopal or Tlotzin,
Or even the still-warm soot of my own father
          Ixtlilxochitl
     (glorious, immortal, but quite unhappy &
          altogether lacking in luck),

& if I continue this catalogue of embarrassing

    questions, tabulating
  the absolute thousands of your illustrious
      ancestors,
What could you say?
For you don't know, you just don't know:
The dust of the first & the dust of the last are now
  - the clay of everyday,
& it's going to happen to us too in just the same way,
& to everybody else, all the people who come after.

MICHAEL S. HARPER

Prayer: Mt. Hood and Environs

The windows of America
are faceless, incestuous screens
pumiced in pure glass,
triangular, innocent,
wired white hoods
cropped in green grass.

Comatose and armed
explorers brought salt water
from the ocean to boil
in three kettles as an offering;

The Indians smoked
on the mountain trails
in buck heat
high along the Columbia;

Lewis and Clark,
their slave, York,

took their salt up
in their webbings;

the meat now cured,
the lumber stink off
the river,
fertilize no soil
without Indian blood
or red roses.

J. C. HOLMAN

from Windsinger

The desert nightwind blows
sand, lamentation
wailing, echoes
or only the howl of a lunatic coyote
learning that he too
is the last of his tribe.

Listen professor
what is survival for a windsinger
without his people?
What good is it to know
the meaning of the stars
if there is no one to tell?
In my spider web lodge
in your suburban badlands
I tend loneliness . . .

Desert nightwind:
I am caretaker
of those sunsets that summoned

the tribe away
into the dark dream
I pass through the trembling mesquite
into those sunsets
becoming my own legend.
I sing.

COLETTE INEZ

Los Quatros Ijadas De Una Palabra

Each word has 4 sides around it
north white west blue
south green east gold
as in the Sioux cosmogony.

Each has direction
as a crow veers
into my eye's circumference

as a chieftain asks the sun
to ride from its cloud.

Cree Zuni Tuscarora Sauk
the continual music

of north jay west shrike
south crane east gull
congruent to the space
which moves their call

Los Quatros Ijadas De Una Palabra: The Four Sides of a Word

over north ice west sand
south loam east stream
moving the word as it pulses.

When a star appears to be fixed
but is roiling
it is a word the one I wanted
to divulge

as love electrifies
the circumscribed sky
in my skull.

ELIZABETH KONOPACKY

Indian Tutoring Collage

Lisa, the Winnebago tongue
could not lick the wounds
festering from your graveled needs
your grandmother didn't speak English good
and your father wasn't a woman
so one day you went off to grow up mute

Joe, gaunt sparrow pecking winter's crumbing eye
you preferred the naked numbness
to borrowed mittens and a foster home
because you are all you will have
and you will not give or take
but die clutching your leeched marrow brown

Dove, your cosmetic veneer imprisoned you
in chic fan mag and nickel cig glamour
as you affectedly swiveled your backside

into the grain of your well-grooved bar stool
but no makeup could harness
your irises streaking red pine knotholes at midnight

Deanna, life is a round deer, whirlpool
coursing on nine lobed feet
and your name is crooked round, too,
those who envisioned only the rims
just saw dizzying circular scrawls
forms out of cornered contexts

Freddy, you only wanted to learn dirty French
so you could make a dent in the myriad places
you never stayed in for long
so you needed a fluid language, Freddy,
of honky-tonk syllables running aimlessly on
and never pausing to mean a word

Robin, you are not that timid bird
but a thunderbird spread flashing
as hovering, swooping, you descend from "Indian
        land"
and you drop wet feathers for Redmen alone
and your headband is a genuine leather thong
cinched talon pulled tight around

Julie, the pelting and buoyant Ma-oo-na's breath
swept you along on its hurtlings
yet your laughter was barefoot prancing in
        rainstorms
and I wished you dripping may flowers
but your footsteps were already ringed
with His august rainbowed eyelids

AL LEE

The Rage of Jackson

[for Arthur Schlesinger, Jr.]

This man's teeth can chew a pine tree down,
but not a hickory. His shoulders bulge
like thunderheads and can lift
up timber. He can wrestle hogs.
Look at the teeth, the ham
of his lips peeled back
by the lumpy fingers of Andrew Jackson.

Undraftable and still at war
with America, the Seminoles
lurk in the secret arms of cypresses
on our perimeters. Congress!
How shall we retrieve our niggers?
By ones and twos into the cuddles
of resistance, they abscond and we
are that much deeper in the bogs of credit.
This man's coarse hair
will crown our flagpole.
His face hardens with a Chinese look
under a slop of skull.

> Top Court Rules
> For Cherokees

"John Marshall has made his decision,
now let him enforce it."

—Jackson on Worcester v. *Georgia*

The people hate a rich man's polished way
of lounging in his sunroom and digesting
a million acres with a signature.
We hate the rich, but when we wake
gaze past the gray horizon and imagine
some Wilderness Road to easy money.
Flailing like a cloud of quarterhorses
westward farther than California,
we flee the rich, just as the Indians
flee the fiery mane of Andrew Jackson.

But . . .

The rich had better keep indoors today.
This is the famous Inauguration:
our boots are muddy
and we spit out the wine on damask.
The President with a shiny knife
can make the dollar dance Jim Crow
and break the Biddle bank.

PHILIP LEGLER

Campos Santo

You can
see them off
the roads, all over
New Mexico,
this one
by the Rio Grande

with names
common as
weeds (Sanchez, Chavez,
Martinez), a
wooden
marker and the bright

bouquets
spring flowers
blooming in plastic
wrappers, and a
knee-high
fence broken down where

the wind's
blown through, to
mark a plot, really
a piece of earth,
as if
in death it was his.

MERIDEL LE SUEUR

I Light Your Streets

I am a crazy woman with a painted face
On the streets of Gallup.
I invite men into my grave
         for a little wine.
I am a painted grave
Owl woman, hooting for callers in the night.
Black bats over the sun sing to me.
The horned toad sleeps in my thighs.
My grandmothers gave me songs to heal
But the white man buys me cheap without song
or word.
My dead children appear and I play with them.
Ridge of time in my grief remembering.
Who will claim the ruins?
      and the graves?
        the corn maiden violated
As the land?
I am a child in my eroded dust.
I remember feathers of the humming bird
and the virgin corn laughing on the cob.
Maize defend me
Prairie wheel around me
I run beneath the guns
      and the greedy eye
and hurricanes of white faces knife me.
But like fox and smoke I gleam among the thrushes
And light your streets.

D. A. LEVY

the bells of the Cherokee ponies

i thought they were
wind chimes
in the streets at night

with my young eyes
i looked to the east
and the distant ringing
of ghost ponies
rose from the ground

Ponies Ponies Ponies

i looked to the east
seeking buddhas to
justify those bells
weeping in the darkness

The Underground Horses
are rising

Cherokee, Delaware, Huron
we will return your land to you

the young horses
will return your land to you
to purify the land
with their tears

The Underground Horses
are rising
to tell their fathers

"In the streets at night
the bells of Cherokee ponies
are weeping."

DICK LOURIE

the Indian on the moon

now that we are ready to go ahead
with another moon shot   as they call it
I saw in the paper that in line with
a new policy of re-focusing
some of our government programs for the
poor   the next astronaut to set foot on
the moon is to be an indian   (as
a group they are reputed to be or to
have been among the most resourceful of
our citizens)   planting the flag of A
merica he will set out to explore—
in that graceful way they seem to have—the
dry seas of his inheritance: that is
the second part of the plan—all of the
other indians are to follow in
the next capsules   we are awarding them
the whole moon: they will rebuild their ancient
cultures in the gray dust   we will look up
to see the thousands of indians as
a spot on the luminous bright disc we
have loved in the sky: and from now on
that indian speck on our lovely moon
will remind us of all our pledges to
them   and now the moon shall be theirs   "as
long as the grass shall grow"   there on the moon.

WALTER LOWENFELS

At Bemidji Falls

Neither spirit nor hawk—
that was my voice you heard
last night by these willows
calling Wacoba, Wacoba

> Yes, this is the secret spring
> the Indians used to visit.
> The woods cover up the sky here;
> it is a sound place to make magic.

> The waterfall
> was there when you were asleep.
> Indians used to trap around the bend.
> Yes, that's the wigwam your ancestor
> blew to hell for a dollar and a half.

Neither wind nor wolf
rustled these willows last night—
that was my blood you heard
calling Wacoba, Wacoba

> I free myself by association—
> I will be Indian,
> a native of Kooch. Give me your blood,
> give me your copper skin, my fathers,
> get me out of this fix!
> Help! I am drowning, Mother,
> drowning in the blood
> I have spilled over these waterfalls.

That was no ghost that moved
last night—that was my heart you heard
under the willows, calling
Wacoba, Wacoba.

HOWARD McCORD

A Day's Journey with Geoffrey Young

pictographs

1) and at the river
   a shape traced on a stone
            the cull of a shape
            by a degenerate hand
   The Shoshoni no Chichimecs

   rude, inglorious, a fish-stink
            heavy as fog.

   No castaway Phoenicians, lost navigators
   Shoshoni and brute, illiterate

   But they danced and knew
            the orgasm
   and ate every day they could.

2) the road to Billy Meadows
            is hardly there anymore

   Buckhorn Creek splits
   and the map doesn't know where anybody is.

   The canyon
   so far and lonely and deep
   exactly
            flight
            and the hands of God

   Bless us
   keep us safe from harm

3)small campsites
   a rabbit femur, some charcoal,
   hardly out of the wind
   They called them the "grass-house people"
   and Bonneville found them "wintering in such
         shelters

                              without roofs, being
                                    merely
                              half circles of brush,
                                    behind
                              which they obtained
                                    but an imperfect
                        protection"

   But this is Nez Percé,
         Sahaptin country,
   the Shoshoni far upstream
   with an "imperfect protection"

         the fall

4)Licentious, vulgar greed
   and the white skin of Satan are not new
   and if Viet Nam is unspeakable
   its total antecedent
   is (in this local space)
         the Treaty of 1855
         violated by the Treaty of 1863
         (the white shits had found gold in the
               Wallowas)
         and the vicious exile 1877–1904
         of Joseph

Nature's gentleman, the ladies could say

(who would not suffer a black hand inside their
        thighs)
a retreat worthy of Xenophon
        "incommoded with women & children"
but the morality of law is power.

5)here the road
    breaks off the crest
        and we've never got to a single place
        and sign said was coming up

The lesson of history, precisely.

            As Standing Bear was denied
            writ of habeas corpus because
            he was not a "person within
            the meaning of the law."
            Reversed 18 April 1877
            but who believed?

the road forks again
and down the one
we did not take is the Master
(always)

the trees see him ride the sound of his drum
going where the dead are afraid to go
prophesying with a spider on his tongue.

            on our road: chukar, three does
            a broken trestle rot-green with moss
            a flat tire, a sinister man
            with his bones on top of his skin,
            and coming up, rain.

The magic we have is that we do not believe in
       magic
and will not retreat.

6)the best thing
    would be to go back to the crest
         camp
    then wait to see what the dawn
    is like from the very top.
    Away from the damned white man
    and the war
    left with just the bones of Indians
    wind
    & the music in your head.

           "The exact nature of Indian
           ownership of land
           appears not to have been understood
           by the early settlers, and the
           misunderstanding was the fruitful
              source
           of trouble and even bloodshed."

There is no way back
       only the disease of our history
       the mutilation of land,
       murder

The Skidi Pawnee gave up a woman to the
       morning star
about corn-planting time

but not every year.

One way is the ten o'clock napalm
absolute possession
a percentage
treachery

"General Jessup, maddened by the public cry
for more energetic action, seized Osceola
and his attendants while holding a conference
under a flag of truce"

beyond

7)The best thing
would be to sit on the ridge
wrapped in a Chilkat blanket
and watch everything go away.

lies
Zyklon-B and C S gas
the constabulary of Grenada,
Mississippi
the torture of children
Lidice and My Lai
Wounded Knee, Hue,
Sand Creek, all
of Quang Ngai Province.

8)We have yet to comprehend
the pilgrimage of Smohalla, prophet
and wanderer of the Sokulk

"he left home secretly
and absented himself for a long time"

On foot to Mexico about 1850
back through Nevada and the spirit land

    messages

       :   : give up the white man :   :
return to trees and stone
and the Dream.

But he knew this country
we look at, Geoff,
and he knew the death that was coming to it
would never go away.

THOMAS McGRATH

from Letter to an Imaginary Friend

. . . A step; a half-step, and a step more, I finally
    make it
Over the shallow lip and stand on the low plateau:
Here's Tommy Comelately to pore over the bones
Another time.
    And what's here—on the little bluff
Over the little river?
    A way station, merely;
A half-way house for the Indian dead—an alphabetic
Boneyard . . .
    It was here the Sioux had a camp on the long
        trail
Cutting the loops of the rivers from beyond the
    Missouri and Mandan
East: toward Big Stone Lake and beyond to the
    Pipestone Quarry.
The place of peace.

A backwoods road of a trail, no tribal
Superhighway; for small bands only. Coming and
        going
They pitched camp here a blink of an eye ago.
It's all gone now—nothing to show for it.
                Skulls
Under the permanent snow of time no wind will lift
Nor shift . . .
                —these drifting bones have entered the rock
                        forever . . .

And all done in the wink of an eye! Why my
        grandmother saw them—
And saw the last one perhaps: ascending the little
        river
On the spring high water in a battered canoe.
                Stole one of her chickens
(Herself in the ark of the soddy with the rifle cocked
        but not arguing)
Took the stolen bird and disappeared into history.

And my father, a boy at Fort Ransom, saw them each
        spring and fall—
Teepees strung on the fallow field where he herded
        cattle.
Made friends and swapped ponies with a boy his own
        age—
And in the last Indian scare spent a week in the old
        fort:
All the soddies abandoned, then.
                Wounded Knee—
The last fight—must have been at that time.
                And now
All: finished.
        South Dakota has stolen the holy
Bones of Sitting Bull to make a tourist attraction!

From Indians we learned a toughness and a strength;
    and we gained
A freedom: by taking theirs: but a real freedom: born
From the wild and open land our grandfathers
    heroically stole.
But we took a wound at Indian hands: a part of our
    soul scabbed over:
We learned the pious and patriotic art of
    extermination
And no uneasy conscience where the man's skin was
    the wrong
Color; or his vowels shaped wrong; or his haircut; or
    his country possessed of
Oil; or holding the wrong place on the map—
    whatever
The master race wants it will find good reasons for
    having . . .

CLARENCE MAJOR

Queen Pamunkey

      An American
in drag but hard as British
morality, in the new
world they, with honor, delivered
themselves, this

twenty-year late crown

to a dead woman. Called her Queen
Anne but her name was chief
Pamunkey.

Grief. She lost Totopotomoi &
the warriors & never forgot nor
forgave. English ends

turned up in the Society for
the Preservation of Virginia.
Richmond 1715.

JOHN R. MILTON

El Turista en El Pueblo

Blanket-wrapped, they stare at me
from sun-washed doorways, shaded
in the permanence of dark
traditions and cool privacy
of adobe rooms. Cubed caverns,
they smell of life and death,
washed only by the sun and moon
and permeated briefly by the sage,
the pine, the baking bread.
Their blankets hang in stillness
on shoulders bent but pure;
passed faces, oiled to brown,
made poignant in neutrality, turn eyes
that pierce the fretful stranger
standing sadly in the rising morning dust.

I wait for recognition
in the deepening wells of old concern;
now I have seen the Pueblo,
breathed new sage and swallowed dust
chipped slowly in a century's winds;
now I have walked where earth
was stirred by a thousand pairs
of shuffling feet, resigned and wise.
The ache is mine alone; they heed it not
but pull the blankets close and turn
to blend again with darkness, melded
shadows in the interiored past.

Adobe walls, five times tiered
to reach the growing sun,

reflect new morning light
o strike me full. Blanketless
I stand exposed, alone, outside,
to think: Fine old traditions
don't come cheap these days:

                              And go.

ROBERT NELSON MOORE, JR.

An Offering to the Dawn Princess

At the rebirth of the moon, my father
packed leaves around brown trout,
put them in the midst of hot stones
and spread their ashes in cooling heaps
to the great wind spirit.

As the snow left, we traveled through the
icy water, moving in the bellies of streams,
seeking the white antelope with eyes
of pink fire. Finally, far into
the country of snakes, we pierced the snowy
body of the doe-goddess and held the
flesh in gently cupping hands. Her eyes
we sealed in leather pouches, holding their power
to our loins like great stones.

My father stayed to die by the bones of the true
princess of dawn, planting branches in the earth
to still its fury at the loss of a virgin daughter.

That was when the spring lay upon me like fur.
Now, the mother land lies sleeping under the
spreading of my fingers,

Blue-eyed women lie naked, staked before my lodge,
burying themselves with screams. I have taken
my pleasure with these daughters of the serpent
river. Their howls filled the night with pleading.

Soon they will dance with flames, their flesh
splitting to the tongues of fire gods slowly turning
them to dreams.

It has come to this: the land of my people, the
land of fleet-moving beasts, the land of sun,
has ceased to cast favor on our bodies.
Our brother the wind no longer breathes his
steely breath in slow pants upon us as we couple
by the sacred river.

We burn the women until their flesh blazes
like crimson eyes spread upon a rock. It is not
enough. Our land escapes and the flesh
of my thighs withers. No son
will learn the chants which would
hold our land together.

We pierce the white breasts,
and braid their streaming hair through
our loins. It blazes yellow in the sun
turning our bodies to metal. The
serpent is upon us. We are forced
to live in rocks like great hunted bears.
Tonight my woman will die, her blood
cooling upon the rocks in pools, uniting
with the blood of white women in the
dust. It will be enough to appease the gods.
It must save us.

MICHAEL MOOS

Cheyenne River Valley

The hooves of the snow buffalo are thudding
Against the dying Dakota prairie.
But beneath the frozen sod, unseen
By the sand blind eyes of dirt farmers,
There are tombs of nomadic hunters,
Water, snail shells pressed into rock.

When the constellations graze the floor of the valley,
Sage leaves break into green flame,
And the grassed hills of sand change to night liquid.
The transparent faces of the Cheyenne dead
Sleep in clay urns,
Floating in a dark river without end.

MIKE NICHOLAS

The Unbuilt Sand Castles of Hawaii

Can you imagine millions of children
Flown by the friendly skies of United,
from alleys, slums, delta flats
From clogged classrooms, sewers
From garbage cans and freight tracks,
Flown to play along these beaches,
Where life runs fresh along the rims . . .
Flown to breathe this blue air,
Where air bubbles explode across eyelids . . .
Flown to pick the fruits of these trees,
Where leaves go about in shades of green . . .
Can you imagine children traveling?

The beaches are now covered with pink meat
Marinated with mai tai and sun-tan lotion
That grease up the sun distant above the waves.
And each day the dead white algae
Creeps down the high-rise;
Some come from far away . . . the 23rd floor . . .
Can you imagine children on the beaches
Instead of this daily dead white algae?
Images are made of children in the sun
Dashing through sun rays into the waves.
Can you imagine children traveling in the Pacific?
Can you imagine children traveling
As if they are simply coming to play?

CHARLES OLSON

Maximus, to Gloucester, Letter 157

        an old Indian chief as hant
        sat on the rock between
        Tarantino's and Mr
        Randazza's and scared the piss out of
        Mr Randazza so he ran back into his
                house

The house I live in, and exactly on the back stairs,
is the sight

of the story
told me by

Mr Misuraca, that,
his mother, reports

that, the whole Fort Section, is
a breeding ground of the ghosts of,

dogs, and that, on those very steps, she saw,
as a girl, a fierce, blue, dog, come at her

as she was going out, the door

        The Tarentines
        were the pests

        of the coast, a bunch of shore Indians
        who raided as far south

        as Gloucester, and were themselves
                conceivably
        parts among the Algonquin people

of them there 1000 AD Wikings:
as these Sicilians

talk an Italian
which is Punic. For the Tarantinos

where Micmacs, first spotted off La Have,
and had been dealing,

before they got down here
as traders with fishermen

since the beginning
of the occupation of the coast

from whom they got
knives and kettles

and coats and then sold them
stolen corn, from peaceful

Indians or shamefully cowardly
Indians who put up with these

Tarentines, huddling in their
shabby huts begging the new-come white
        man to

help them up against this raiding bunch
of old tough remnants of the older

coast. Or they were dogs, the Tarentinos,
come in to feed on the after coast,

after the white man disease
—the yellowing disease,

the Indians themselves called

what no man yet has diagnosed,

       except that Indians,
who had been hauled,

to London,
seem somewhere,

to have brought it
back. These Tarentines

were intrusions
on all the coast, east

of Penobscot Bay

RONALD OVERTON

Found Poems

I Indian Un-horsed

The Indians were wonderful
bareback riders—
but the superior weapons
of our Western Pioneers
overcame the native skill and cunning
of the red savages.

Here we see an Indian
shot right off his wild horse.

II Ambush!

The lonely pioneer
was plodding his lonesome way
along the floor of the Canyon,
when the sudden sound

of a rolling pebble
caused him to wheel around.
                              There
on top of the cliff
hostile Indians lay in ambush.

The white man shot twice
and two red-skins bit the dust!

III   Doe-Wah-Jack

A very hardy Indian was Doe-Wah-Jack
and renowned for his fortitude.

In praying to the Great Spirit
he would go as long as four days
without eating,
or drinking
or sleeping.

IV   Ma-Ta-He-Hah

They called him "Old Bear"
because he was the mystery medicine man
of the Mandan tribe.

All the herbs in the forest were known to him,
and many a baby Indian's stomach trouble
did he cure with his rhubarb roots
and sulphur solutions.

V   Geronimo

Before this Apache war lord

was finally captured by the Federal troops
and put in prison, many
were the bloody, vicious raids he made
in New Mexico and Arizona.

He was captured once before by General Cook,
but cunningly managed to escape.

Not so lucky the second time, he
languished in prison until the end of his days.

GUY OWEN

Who Speaks For The Red Man?

Who speaks for the Red Man
Now the black man's found a tongue:
Chippewa, Hopi, Sioux,
Seminole, Lumbee, Ute?

Who lifts their heroes in song:
Crazy Horse, Tecumseh, Joseph,
Black Hawk, Little Wolf, Philip?

The sacred hoop is broken,
The prayer feathers scattered,
The kivas are empty
        and desolate as the watering holes of buffalo,

Still: a wind is rising like a cry
        from Wounded Knee,
In pathless woods an owl scrapes at the dark . . .
Listen: in the veins of earth comes a throbbing
        like muted drums
        that will never cease.

MARGE PIERCY

Curse of the earth magician on a metal land

Marching, a dream of wind in our chests,
a dream of thunder in our legs,
we tied up midtown Manhattan for half an hour,
the Revolutionary Contingent and Harlem,
but it did not happen
because it was not reported in any newspaper.
The riot squad was waiting at the bottom of 42nd
        Street
to disperse us into uncertain memory.
A buffalo said to me
I used to crop and ruminate on LaSalle Street in
        Chicago
and the grasses were sweet under the black tower of
        the Board of Trade.
Now I stand in the zoo next to the yaks.
Let the ghosts of those recently starved rise
and like piranhas in ten seconds flat chew down to
        public bones
the generals and the experts on anti-personnel
        weapons
and the senators and the oil men and the lobbyists
and the sleek smiling sharks who dance at the
        Diamond Ball.
I am the earth magician about to disappear into the
        ground.
This is butterfly's war song about to disappear into
        the fire
Put the eagle to sleep.
I see from the afternoon papers
that we have bought another country

and are cutting the natives down to build jet
      airstrips.
A common motif in monumental architecture in the
      United States
is an eagle with wings spread, beak open
and the glove grasped in his claws.
Put the eagle to sleep.
This is butterfly's war song addressed to the Congress
      of Sharks.
You are too fat, you eat bunches of small farmers like
      radishes for breakfast.
You are rotting your teeth with sugar
refined from the skulls of Caribbean children. Thus
      far
we have only the power of earth magicians, dream
      and song and marching,
to dance the eagle to sleep.
We are about to disappear into the fire.
There is only time for a brief curse by a chorus of
      ghosts
of Indians murdered with smallpox and repeating
      rifles on the plains,
of Indians shot by the marines in Santo Domingo,
napalmed in the mountains of Guatemala last week.
There will be no more spring.
Your corn will sprout in rows and the leaves will
      lengthen
but there will be no spring running clean water
      through the bones,
no soft wind full of bees, no long prairie wind
      bearing feathers of geese.
It will be cold or hot. It will step on your necks.
A pool of oil will hang over your cities,
oil slick will scum your lakes and streams killing the
      trout and the ducklings,

concrete and plastic will seal the black earth and the
      red earth,
your rivers hum with radioactivity and the salmon
      float belly up,
and your mountains be hollowed out to hold the files
      of great corporations,
and shale oil sucked from under the Rockies till the
      continent buckles.
Look! children of the shark and the eagle
you have no more spring. You do not mind.
You turn on the sunlamp and the airconditioning
and sit at the television watching the soldiers dance.

DAVID RAY

The Indians Near Red Lake

When the white man comes
he comes to see a grave,
to look at the little house
over the grave, to ask
how the dead can eat the food
placed there
and always we give him the same answer
"The same way, white man,
your dead can smell your flowers."

The white man is interested
only in death.
He cares nothing for the story
of the pregnant girls
digging the banana-shaped roots

of the yellow lily
with their toes, tucking one
in at the waist for good luck.

The white man wants to hear
about the German scalp
brought back in nineteen forty-five.
He wants to hear how
it was put on the Chief's grave
after three nights of scalpdance.
He is amused
to think the Chief may stroll
in the other world
with the Germans and the small Japanese
for servants.

He walks through the weeds of our yards
to see a grave.
He brings nothing
else, none of the friendship,
the fellowship we've spread our nets for
for years, in our yards,
beside the abandoned Buicks,
waiting for him to notice.

The nets go on catching spiders
and what the white man throws away as
he drives through, fast,
in his car.
We take our smiles to town
but neither do they catch anything.
Our nets are dry.
Yet we watch them.

ADRIENNE RICH

8/1/68

The order of the small town on the riverbank,
forever at war with the order of the dark and starlit
    soul.

We you free then all along, Jim, free at last,
of everything by the white boy's fantasies?

We pleaded guilty till we saw what rectitude was
    like:
its washed hands, and dead nerve, and sclerotic eye.

I long ago stopped dreaming of pure justice, your
    honor—
my crime was to believe we could make cruelty
    obsolete.

The body has been exhumed from the burnt-out
    bunker;
the teeth counted, the contents of the stomach told
    over.

And you, Custer, the Squaw-killer, hero of primitive
    schoolrooms—
where are you buried, what is the condition of your
    bones?

B. H. ROGERS

from The Man Above the Land

"Heyna" the son
of an Omaha
Sioux whose
fathers
unceremoniously
will bury him in
potter's field
       doesn't look to the sky
above the Winnebago Indian school mission
he doesn't pray to his God or roam over
the prairies; the house of his children;
he is beyond being a broken man
     as wild rice scattered from the chaff
that's broken and scattered by the wind
       "Heyna" is on the high
road he's flying   fly
fly like seed pods into
gourds that turn yellow and grow hard in the land

MICHAEL RUMAKER

Poem

Indians, stop interrupting my dreams—
    Let me sleep the white death.
Blacks, stop interrupting my sleep—
    Dream my dead whiteness
       back in my/your body.
      My death is to stop time
    To shut my eyes to space
      (forgive me, Charles)
       the vast alkaline
       light of the west
      blinds me with fear.
I kill it with a bending inward
     as my fathers killed you
who moved with grace and assurance
     in that space
      that land
  we have never loved
except for what we have stolen from it
  and never put back anything
    but sludge.
I, the son, dream murderous dreams.
    I, the son, ache to be
   taken back into the land again,
    into the blood-rich soil
    that cracked your feet
     and held you close, open,
      alive.

RUTH LISA SCHECHTER

Along Missouri

             on cradleboards of America
language
leaped to prairie and spruce root
in deer hoofs like castanets to
         South Dakota sunrise beaded
Indian necklace on forehead from girl to squaw
    NAVAHO on forehead traveling
      APACHE southwest over desert
on small   Spanish horses
shearing   seed   digging
fine arrowhead
chipped to a point
        On cradleboard of American tent-
dwelling marriage   along Missouri
dancing in raven mask   and grizzly bear
         CEREMONY FOR FIRE
we inherited
the language   the free verse   daring
lightning poetry
singing no tune Chinook   and buffalo bleeding
near feathers of   GREAT SPIRITS
dying through
Hollywood movie finale
hunter and slave   THE EPIC FILM   of Cecil B.
DeMille   on a fiddle waltzing
in snapshots and lilies
        Were they cruel
in willow boats
signalling   PERMIT PEACE?
yet   Iroquois sons and daughters   were safe
from Iroquois warriors   safe from the civilized
shooting them down

              to lie dreaming   mouth open
on university green   left   right
Tuscaloosa   Mississippi   Ohio   where
we sent our children
with sunflower faces   believing
history of   Patrick Henry with Jefferson
blessing   we sent our children   enchanted
pledging their blood   their allegiance
on arrows and alphabets
                    on cradleboards of America
chipped
in free speech.

RAY SMITH

A Fragment for Last Pony of the Dacotah

That was our country, the Four Winds know it,
From Bear Butte through the hills to where you have
    named Montana.
My own people stayed out with Rain-in-the-Face
When others untied the knots in their ponies' tails
And went in as Three Star said to the reservation.

This was the winter before Longhair's coming.

The snow came, the first heavy snow,
White everywhere, but the river dark and whirling.
That was an empty time, the women glum,
The tepee hunger-silent, no cooking smell,
But parched corn eaten under the buffalo robe.

I went to hunt with Crow-That-Does Not-Fly.
This was my wearing, buckskin, but no coat,
No hat or mittens like I'm wearing now.

On foot, the second day we found the track of deer
And followed all day, lurching in the snow.
Near dark we saw the buck under a tree
Nose down to scuff the snow. Crow-That-Does-Not-Fly
Shot his one-bullet gun, and I an arrow.
While it thrashed we ran up with drawn knives
And slit the belly first to warm our hands.
That coming back was slow, the deer frozen heavy,
But soon enough laughter filled our tepees.
Even the wrinkles of Small Bear, my mother's father,
Smoothed out as he lighted his pipe with vigor.
"Make a feast," he said. "Put some taste in all this
          woodsmoke!"

Other times we starved, waiting for spring.

A Crow war party stole one night through a
          snowstorm
And drove six ponies back over the Rosebud.
Fast Elk called me through the tent-flap
"Hurry with weapons!" I seized my bear-tooth
          necklace
(My war medicine) and took my bow and knife.

Outside there was shouting in the first gray light,
Men and horses dim in the snowfall. Fast Elk,
The party leader, brought my pony up.
He said "This will shake the sleep out of your eyes!"
Seven of us plunged west, the village waking behind
          us.
Soon we rode in a moving cloud of snow
Single file. We crossed where the Rosebud narrows.
I felt the icy splash upon my ankle.
Our thighs aching with cold we rode,
The horses faltering sometimes in the drift,
Their steaming breath whirled with the windy snow.

WILLIAM STAFFORD

People Who Went by in Winter

The morning man came in to report
that something had crossed the field
in the night during the storm. He heard
ribbons of wind snap at their tether
and a sound like some rider saying
the ritual for help, a chant or a song.
When we went out all we found
were deep, slow tracks in freezing mud
and some sticks tied together hanging
from the lowest branch of the oldest
tree by the river.

While beginning snow eddied and curtained
thicker and thicker, on, we looked,
The grass hurried by, seething, then silent,
brown, all the way to the west, a little
touch-by-touch trail to the mountains.
Our boss turned back: "No.
We can't help them. They sing till
they find a place to winter. They have
tents. They make it, somehow." He
looked off that long way, where
the grass tossed.

Riding home, he told us:
"My people were like them,
over around Grand Prairie—slaves once,
then landowners. Now they pass like
this, and I heard them, because
I wake up and am partly theirs."

He looked at every man, and
he put his hand on the neck of his horse:
"They are our people, yours and mine,
all of us," he said.
"In every storm I hear them pass."

STAN STEINER

But, the Africans Walked at Night

But, the Africans walked at night
to Lukachukai
to Tohatchi
to Chinle
in the sacred groves of graves of the peach trees
of Kit Carson,
                  the father,
of death.

But, the Africans walked at night
succoring the Earth Mother.

But, the Africans walked at night
the lawyers of Ibo and Kikuyu
wondering where are the warrior
sons.

    Come to feast!
    on unleavened bread
    and governmental
    beasts
            to eat
    tribal fables
    mouthed by TV

tubes full of
Last Suppers
of Cheeseburgers—

But, the Africans walked at night
black as Christs
shrouded
in whiteskinned
business suits of cellophane and aluminum foil
under the moon
of the coyote.

But, the Africans walked at night
in Italian shoes.

But, the Africans walked at night
through dark light
to uranium women
in unlit hogans
who welcomed them blindly
to the way of beauty.

But, the Africans walked at night
medicine bags and stone balls
in their attaché cases.

    Where the warriors
    lie in motels
    of the Navajos
    eyeing redhanded
    knives of yellow
    butter eaters
    the blunted spears
    of the eunuched
        Indians—
But, the Africans walked at night

wondering where
John Wayne was hiding
his red cosmetics—
why Gary Cooper shot
Pocahontas—
                    why
the warriors of Jeff Chandler
washed their wounds white
with detergents

But, the Africans walked at night
to wickiups with beautyrest beds.

But, the Africans walked at night
to exercise
tours of diplomacy
with the State
departmentalized guides who dreamt of reddest sex
frozen in ice cream cones of blackest secrets.

But, the Africans walked at night
four hundred miles
of years of death
marched to wars
across the deserts
of history to be buried
with unborn Indians
in concentration camps
of the Army of Christ.

But, the Africans walked at night
disguised as one million dead Indians, yelling,
Uruhu!

GENEVIEVE TAGGARD

The Luau

Odor of algarroba, lure of release,
The smell of red lehua and the crisp scent of
      maile . . .
These words and images will help you after a little.
Hypnotic words emerge and bloom in the mind,
Anaesthetic names . . . Dry buzz of bees
Who make a honey eaten at early breakfast
From a comb like a broken coral . . .
Do dreams foretell the honey? Break the spell.

So I come home in the valley of Kalihi,
My bare feet on hard earth, hibiscus with
      stamen-tongue
Twirled in my fingers like a paper windmill,
A wheel of color, crimson, the petals large,
Kiss of the petal, tactile, light intense . . .

Now I am back again, I can touch the children:
My human race, in whom was a human dwelling,
Whose names are all the races—of one skin.
For so our games ran tacit, without blur.

What brings me back with giant steps to them?
What was the feast that woke this fabulous thirst?
What was the summer fruit we found and ate
Boldly, with the children of Adam?

A game and a daily search
In the harvest of trees. We played a parable.
We possessed a valley, devoured the juicy, dense

Jewels of appetite hung in fresco sweeps,
In garlands and in fountains toward the sea.
Mangoes of golden flesh, with turpentine
Peel and odor. Cut plums of inky stain
And the pucker of persimmons. Dates to be got
By stepping up a tree trunk. Coconuts
with custard centers. Rose and custard apple,
Eugenia, pink, lemon and little orange,
Guava seedy and tart, and the hidden poha,
And the sacklike fig, to be ripped, to be seen, to be
       tasted.
How rasping sweet the suck of sugar cane—
Papaya and banana taken for granted.

With giant steps, in sleep and troubled pain
I return to the fabulous fear, the old communion,
With bodiless hunger and thirst. Why have I come
Away from the adult world where race is war?

Here we are dipping and passing the calabash
In a ceremony of friends; I also;
But in frenzy and pain distort
the simple need, knowing how blood is shed:
                              To sit together

Drinking the blue ocean, eating the sun
Like a fruit . . .

QUINCY TROUPE

Red Bone Pot Lunch

California/L. A. sun people
beating down my black singing days
into the blood fusion
comes the rhythm of their poems
wheeling far-out over wide
spaced days comes the
image-song blending
sun/sea-salt spray

the music in salt waves

where days pass when one thinks
the entire beautiful world of long
legged bikini-clad super-bad ladies
tan their black
brown/yellow/pink-bodies
beneath an eye-balling sun
on the burning-shifting sands
of Malibu Beach

& the days burn drifting
piling years, as freezing Wyoming snow
drifts during winter; as snow-cold
froze the grotesque twisted body
of Big Foot, at the battle
of Wounded Knee

But there are many sorry specters who will
                                        tell you

that all the bleeding days passing through

their sick sterile worlds, are as beautiful

as all the beautiful ladies
tanning on Malibu Beach

CHARLIE VERMONT

Dream

(for Bill)

I cut the cyst out
from above my right eye
it was nothing, a simple operation
as soon as I touched it with the knife
it popped out and to my surprise
it was only an Indianhead nickel
with skin over it

MARK VINZ

Dakota Death Song

Third moon of the third season.
The evening elms have summoned them,
ancestors, chanting the colors of their death.

They come now
disguised in the fiery hooves of buffalo,
hidden in the talons of hunter owls.

I am discovered
crouching on the floor of an abandoned lake,
and the rooms of my body are crowded
with their spirit eyes.

Old men
spilling their dead seed across startled pores
the ancient hands of women
plucking the voice from its throat.

Tendons separate,
the cage of bones is opened—
flayed skin drying on the ridgepoles
of the night.

And now the scalping knife,
the lonely blade edge
dropping from the sunrise like a sigh:
      child, where are you,
      blood of our blood,
      flesh of our flesh!

MARNIE WALSH

John Knew-The-Crow
(Fort Yates, North Dakota, 1880)

I saw a blue winged bird
sitting silent in the marsh,
his brothers flown away.
Ice grew among his feathers.

I saw a snake
in the forest rock.
She gave me warning, I gave her none;
I wear hers against my breast.

I saw the buffalo in rut.
They could not see me
for the earth ran away into the sky,
and the sound carried off the sun.

I saw the turtle on the grass,
too big, too blind to move.
His neck died beneath my ax,
but the claws walked on toward the water.

I saw my mother and my father die,
and the soldiers took me away.

WILLIAM WANTLING

Initiation

20 years after cubscouts
WEBELOS returned for me
carried me up Stone Mountain
under the purple double-dome
left me there
on the 3rd day I saw her
etched into the window of my hut
& she was hawk, she was eagle
hanging the edge of a red & dying
              sun
black, hanging, poised
then wheeling, diving the void
screamed down upon me
clutched me
we were one
carried us up, up above the
              sun
into the no-longer-dying
light, ah the light

why should I return?

RAMONA WEEKS

An Aleutian Illusion

Beneath a cairn I slept on stepping stones,
on the long arm flailing in sadness, on the Aleutians
I lived there, decoying the otter with fog

and hoping for the old poryishki
to come, ringing the doorbells of sleep.
It is too early now for the sun.

Ivory shows its youth to the wolverines.
It bares its portcullis blaze in
shell middens that crouch by the strait.

I set out upon my oblivion's
task. Knocking about with narwhals, I answer
only crowning blows, lost in their royal

horned haze. We seek a snail that drips purple,
its blood dyeing the arachnid beach,
strewn with the masts of old clippers

carved near the Clyde or the Amyr.
"I am here," shrieks the telegraph glass
insulator, buried in soup and the wrestled

shell hairpins of elderly reindeer.
"Where?" asks the polar bear, enamored of messages.
Between them the borealis flutters

like auklets chained by their nostrils
or lemmings swimming hard in the tides. Light fails
and time grieves in my thumbs,

whizzing fishline bearing the initials
of Rosicrucians to unbelievers who smack
of their heresy deep in the sea.

Borne of silver salvers of winter, the drowned
gasp by, filibustering rhetoricians
out of their element, caught in the cold

where it snaps like brutal elastic
out of the north. I am your snow
doppelganger, closer than a snakeskin of ice,

chained to your roots and taking over
as bells do, eliminating my rivals,
turning a dark blue face to my northern

papa, saying, "This man who alternates
joy with seed pearls and claptrap must share
my throne with me." My papa has pale

hirelings who ready the coach and the four
corners of the world. By quadrangles we rust
toward our whitest corners and our densest poles.

The undulant grotto of the Aleutians is
the clawed hand of our receiver. Banked
by ice hearths we learn to love burning.

ANNA WHITE FEATHER

Near Tassajara Bon Owl—to be sung

eyes like these neither give off nor receive energy
I know this condition well
it has affected me all of my life
it is very dangerous
you cannot know of the existence of the scorpion
until after he bites

you ask if a child is born out of shit
the answer is
that the child is surrounded by hot blood
and heartbeat
that is why
we now play drums around this fire

Julian is a beautiful name
so is Rachel the child, wearing a necklace of yarn
Ira-Ora-Aura   Leah means wild cow
with feather masks more delicate than air
Julian and Rachel the child eat together
the graceful fruits of Earth
o dark Mother primordial
devour us not

vernal:
all the little children love peppermint tea
and angelica
allah dada
allah dada

I thank that which is invisible and which I don't
          understand.
I thank this language.

Perceived word-for-word this is but ceremonial food
    for the dead.
So do not be deluded, but know this form-by-spirit
and the energy in these hollow bones will not elude
    you.

NANCY WILLARD

I can remember
when there were trees

I can remember when there were trees,
great tribes of spruces who deckled themselves in
    light,
beeches buckled in pewter, meeting like Quakers,
the golden birch, all cutwork satin,
courtesan of the mountains; the paper birch
trying all summer to take off its clothes
like the swaddlings of the newborn.

The hands of a sassafras blessed me,
I saw maples fanning the fire in their stars,
heard the coins of the aspens rattling like teeth,
saw cherry trees spraying fountains of light,
smelled the wine my heel pressed from ripe apples,
saw a thousand planets bobbing like bells
on the sleeve of the sycamore, chestnut, and lime.

The Algonquins knew that a tree is worthy of
    worship,
A few wise men from their tribe broke through the
    sky,
climbing past worlds to come and the rising moon
on the patient body of the tree of life,
and brought back the souls of the newly slain,

no bigger than apples, and dressed the tree
as one of themselves and danced.

Even the conquerors of this country
lifted their eyes and found the trees
more comely than gold: *Bright green trees,*
the whole land so green it is pleasure to look on it,
and the greatest wonder to see the diversity.
During that time, I walked among trees,
the most beautiful things I had ever seen.*

Watching the shadows of trees, I made peace with
        mine.
Their forked darkness gave motion to morning light.
Every night the world fell to the shadows,
and every morning came home, the dogwood floating
its petals like moons on a river of air,
the oak kneeling in wood sorrel and fern,
the willow washing its hair in the stream.

And I saw how the logs from the mill floated
downstream, saw otters and turtles that rode them,
and though I heard the saws whine in the woods,
I never thought men were stronger than trees.
I never thought those tribes would join their brothers,
the buffalo and the whale, the leopard, the seal, the
        wolf,
and the men of this country who knew how to sing
        them.

Nothing I ever saw washed off the sins of the world
so well as the first snow dropping on trees.

* From Columbus's journals, as adapted by William Carlos
Williams.

We shoveled the pond clear and skated under their
      branches,
our voices muffled in their huge silence.
The trees were always listening to something else.
They didn't hear the beetle with the hollow tooth
grubbing for riches, gnawing for empires, for gold.

Already the trees are a myth,
half gods, half giants, in whom nobody believes.
But I am the oldest woman on earth,
I can remember when there were trees.

KEITH WILSON

Koyemsi

Those mudheads. Dancing
clowns, born of brother
& sister mating. Eaters
of feces.

Splayed feet. Mud
between the toes, clay
masks & bodies

—humor, insanity
  remain, in them,
  sacred

& these gods are not
under masks, watch
out of the wind
rain growing corn.

Children, children
with pollen in their mouths
laughing, please them,
koyemsi, risen from earth

they who led the People
from the Underworld, risen
from deep clay, the singing
shines in their victory, rite

a celebration of horrors conquered
by dancing feet & laughter, mica
particles flashing out of clay
the laughter comes, dancing.

PHILIP WOFFORD

The Old and the Young Dance Separately

Pueblo kids in feathers sprayed day-glo
stomp high-kneed in woolworth leggings—
flashing dancers on leave from Indian School
stomp once more through dust and stop.

> Old woman selling bowls
> on ceremonial day explains,
> wears turquoise and silver
> like medals of endurance,
> explains marks she made in clay:
> "This is mountain,
> this bird,
> this lightning.
> It has always been so."

Then, the old men begin moving,
out of mist they shuffle
in worn work clothes they move
as if just crossing a phantom distance
to take their turn with earth and sky.

        The bright-winged kids
        stand jiving with cokes
        and portable rock,
        resting, watching,
        at the crowd's edge,
        waiting to get back in,
        to stomp and shake dust
        like clouds of gunsmoke.

It takes a long, long time for the old men
to move in their small half circle
from one end of the pueblo to the other,
it takes time for their voices to reach us,
for their hands to shape the air and give it bodied
      spirit.

        All day
        the dance changes,
        fast, then slow—
        bright young, grey old—
        both so beautiful,
        so separate, atop
        the high pile of stone,
        their home,
        where nothing grows.

The old and the young dance separately,
and move with the sun's arc into darkness.
      They meet somewhere we do not see.

Traditional Indian Poems

Introduction

RARIHOKWATS*

Words can be translated, but the settings, the speakers, the situations are all left behind. We can spend a half-hour or more shuffling in a circle singing over and over words which translate simply to "It is nice! It is nice!" with great spiritual esthetic (poetic?) satisfaction—something very impossible to do in English, and completely impossible to reduce to print. It is the poetic experience that counts, not the poetry.

No one who has experienced the strength of the words of our Grandparents will be satisfied to see that power reduced to a strange language, metered neatly in sterile lines of unfeeling words. The richness of the ceremonial life, the security of having emerged from this land, surrounded by your people, give words uttered by loved elders meaning which their literate renderings can only hint.

Thoughts that have endured for so many tens of thousands of years still live because they are alive, renewed with each passing turn of the cycles. And they are meant to live, not be "preserved." The poetry of the People lingers in the morning mists and is painted on the land by every setting sun. It is poetry stirred by the Mysteries of Life, whispered by the winds and waters—anyone who knows the Creation can find it there, and voice it from the silence of his being.

For those whose lives have lost primitive (primary) meaning, the translations of the Ancients into English may be as close as they will get to knowing what it means to be a part of this land and life. They are to the real poetry what a travel-agency folder is to the journey itself—a well-dressed but pale abstraction that leaves a wistful thought that someday you too might have this experience.

Listen to the words of your Grandmother, the Moon. It was she who taught the people the Night Chant.

* Rarihokwats is a member of the Bear Clan of the Mohawk Nation at Akwesasne. He edits *Akwesasne Notes,* a newspaper of native affairs published at Rooseveltown, New York, 13683.
Akwesasne is the Mohawk word for "where the partridge drums."

Listen to the Grandfathers, the Thunderers. It is they who sing the Horse Song the best.

Fast, and sit in silence in a sacred spot. Let your heart teach you to lament for your sons.

Talk to the trees and caress their leaves. Find the words to thank them for their beauty, their shade, their fruit, their shelter.

Become a part of the winds. Go where they go, rustle the grass and bring the rains. Cleanse the air, and return to tell your people where you have been.

In ways such as these, you will voice the poetry of the Creation, the traditional poetry of the Native Peoples. It is in the hearts of the people that the poetry is placed to live.

We are your Grandchildren, Ancient Ones! Speak to us!

HHE-THA-A-HI: Eagle Wing

Dated 1881

My brothers, the Indians, must always be remembered in this land. Out of our languages we have given names to many beautiful things which will always speak of us. Minnehaha will laugh at us, Seneca will shine in our image, Mississippi will murmur our woes. The broad Iowa and the rolling Dakota and the fertile Michigan will whisper our names to the sun that kisses them. The roaring Niagara, the sighing Illinois, the singing Delaware, will chant unceasingly our Dat-wa-e (Death Song). Can it be that you and your children will hear that eternal song without a stricken heart? We have been guilty of only one sin—we have had possessions that the white man coveted. We moved away toward the setting sun; we gave up our homes to the white man.

My brethren, among the legends of my people it is told how a chief, leading the remnant of his people, crossed a great river, and striking his tepee-stake upon the ground, exclaimed, "A-la-ba-ma!" This in our language means "Here we may rest!" But he saw not the future. The white man came: he and his people could not rest there; they were driven out, and in a dark swamp they were thrust down into the slime and killed. The word he so sadly spoke has given a name to one of the white man's states. There is no spot under those stars that now smile upon us where the Indian can plant his foot and sigh "A-la-ba-ma." It may be that Wakanda will grant us such a place. But it seems that it will be only at His side.

ABENAKI

The Parted Lovers

THE MAN SINGS

My parents think they can separate me
from the girl I love;
We have vowed to love each other while
we live.
Their commands are vain: we shall see
each other while the world lasts.
Yes!   let them say or do what they like;
we shall see each other while the rocks
stand.

THE WOMAN SINGS

Here I sit on this point, whence I can see
the man that I love.
Our people think that they can sever us;
but I shall see him while the world
lasts.
Here shall I remain, in sight of the one
I love.

—Translated by John Reade

APACHE

Songs of the Masked Dancers

I.

When the earth was made;
When the sky was made;
When my songs were first heard;
The holy mountain was standing toward me with
      life.

At the center of the sky, the holy boy walks four ways
      with life.
Just mine, my mountain became; standing toward me
      with life.
Gan* children became; standing toward me with life.

When the sun goes down to the earth,
Where Mescal Mountain lies with its head toward the
      sunrise,
Black spruce became; standing up with me.

2.

Right at the center of the sky the holy boy with life
      walks in four directions.
Lightning with life in four colors comes down four
      times.

The place which is called black spot with life;
The place which is called blue spot with life;
The place which is called yellow spot with life;
The place which is called white spot with life;

* The Apache call their Masked Dancers "Gan."

They have heard about me,
The black Gans dance in four places.
The sun starts down toward the earth.

3.

The living sky black-spotted;
The living sky blue-spotted;
The living sky yellow-spotted;
The living sky white-spotted;
The young spruce as girls stood up for their dance in
     the way of life.
When my songs first were, they made my songs with
     words of jet.
Earth when it was made,
Sky when it was made,
Earth to the end,
Sky to the end,
Black Gan, black thunder, when they came toward
     each other,
The various bad things that used to be vanished.
The bad wishes which were in the world vanished.
The lightning of black thunder struck four times for
     them.
It struck four times for me.

4.

When first my songs became,
When the sky was made,
When the earth was made,
The breath of the Gans on me made only of down;
When they heard about my life;

Where they got their life;
When they heard about me;
It stands.

5.

The day broke with slender rain.
The place which is called "lightning's water stands,"
The place which is called "where the dawn strikes,"
Four places where it is called "it dawns with life,"
I land there.
The sky boys, I go among them.
He came to me with long life.
When he talked over my body with the longest life,
The voice of thunder spoke well four times.
Holy sky boy spoke to me four times.
When he talked to me my breath became.

—Translated by Pliny Earle Goddard

CHEROKEE

To Destroy Life

Listen! Now I have come to step over your
    soul.
You are of the Wolf clan.
Your name is A'yu'nini.
Your spittle I have put at rest under the
    earth.
I have come to cover you over with the
    black rock.
I have come to cover you over with the
    black cloth.
I have come to cover you over with the
    black slabs, never to reappear.
Toward the black coffin of the upland in
    the Darkening Land your paths shall
    stretch out.
So shall it be for you.
The clay of the upland has come to cover
    you.
Instantly the black clay has lodged there
    where it is at rest at the black houses
    in the Darkening Land.
With the black coffin and with the black
    slabs I have come to cover you.
Now your soul has faded away.
It has become blue.
When darkness comes your spirit shall
    grow less and dwindle away, never to
    reappear.
Listen!

—Translated by James Mooney

DWAMISH

Chief Seattle Speaks*

"When the last Red man shall have become a myth
    among
                the White men,
when your children's children find themselves alone
    in the field, the store, upon the highway, or in
    the pathless woods,
they will not be all alone.
In all the earth there is no place dedicated to
    solitude.
At night when the streets of your cities are silent and
    you
                think them deserted,
they will throng with the returning hosts that once
    filled them
                and still fill this beloved land.
The White man will never be alone.

Let him be just and deal kindly with my people, for
    the dead
                are not powerless.
Dead—I say?
There is no death. Only a change of worlds."

* This was Chief Seattle's speech to Isaac Stevens, Governor of
Washington Territory, in 1854.

SOUTHERN CALIFORNIA

The Eagle's Song

Said the Eagle:
>   I was astonished
>   When I heard that there was death.
>
>   My home, alas,
>   Must I leave it!
>   Summits that see all
>   Shall I see you no more!
>
>   North I went,
>   Leaning on the wind;
>   Through the forest resounded
>   The cry of the hunted doe.
>
>   East I went,
>   Through the hot dawning;
>   There was the smell of death in my nostrils.
>
>   South I went, seeking
>   The place where there is no death.
>   Weeping I heard
>   The voice of women
>   Wailing for their children.
>
>   West I went,
>   On the world encompassing water;
>   Death's trail was before me.
>
>   People, O people,
>   Needs be that we must die!

Therefore let us make
Songs together.
With a twine of songs to bind us
To the middle Heaven,
The white way of souls.
There we shall be at rest,
With our songs
We shall roam no more!

—Reexpressed by Mary Austin

CHIPPEWA

My Love Has Departed

A loon,
I thought it was.
But it was
My love's
Splashing Oar.

—Translated by Frances Densmore

HAVASUPAI

Sun, my relative

Sun, my relative
Be good coming out
Do something good for us.

Make me work,
So I can do anything in the garden
I hoe, I plant corn, I irrigate.

You, sun, be good going down at sunset
We lay down to sleep I want to feel good.

While I sleep you come up.
Go on your course many times,
Make good things for us men.

Make me always the same as I am now.

IROQUOIS

Death of a Son

My son!

Listen once more
to the words of your mother.

You were brought into life
with her pains.
You were nourished
with her life.
She has attempted to be faithful
in raising you up.
When you were young
she loved you
as her life.
Your presence has been a source
of great joy to her.
Upon you she depended
for support and comfort
in her declining days.
She had always expected
to gain the end of the path of life
before you.
But you have outstripped her,
and gone before her.

Our great and wise creator
has ordered it so.

Your friends and relatives
have gathered about your body,

to look upon you
for the last time.
We mourn, as with one mind,
your departure from us.
We too have but a few days more
before we take the same path.

It is no longer possible
for us to walk together.
We release you for your journey.
Do not let the things of this earth
hinder you.
Do not let your friends
trouble your mind.
Regard none of these things.

These are all my words, my son.

—Translated by Ely S. Parker

MESCALERO APACHE

Dawn Song

(from the Gotal Ceremony)

The black turkey in the east spreads his tail
The tips of his beautiful tail are the white dawn

Boys are sent running to us from the dawn
They wear yellow shoes of sunbeams

They dance on streams of sunbeams

Girls are sent dancing to us from the rainbow
They wear shirts of yellow

They dance above us the dawn maidens

The sides of the mountains turn to green
The tops of the mountains turn to yellow

And now above us on the beautiful mountains it is
dawn.

—Translated by Pliny Earle Goddard

NAVAJO

A Prayer of the Night Chant

Tsegihi,
House made of dawn,
House made of evening light.
House made of the dark cloud.
House made of male rain.
House made of dark mist.
House made of female rain.
House made of pollen.
House made of grasshoppers.
Dark cloud is at the door.
The trail out of it is dark cloud.
The zigzag lightning stands high upon it.
Male deity!
Your offering I make.
I have prepared a smoke for you.
Restore my feet for me.
Restore my legs for me.
Restore my body for me.
Restore my mind for me.
This very day take out your spell for me.
Your spell remove for me.
You have taken it away for me.
Far off it has gone.
Happily I recover.
Happily my interior becomes cool.
Happily I go forth.
My interior feeling cool, may I walk.
No longer sore, may I walk.
Impervious to pain, may I walk.
With lively feelings may I walk.

As it used to be long ago, may I walk.
Happily may I walk.
Happily, with abundant dark clouds, may I walk.
Happily, with abundant showers, may I walk.
Happily, with abundant plants, may I walk.
Happily, on a trail of pollen, may I walk.
Happily may I walk.
Being as it used to be long ago, may I walk.
May it be beautiful before me.
May it be beautiful behind me.
May it be beautiful below me.
May it be beautiful above me.
May it be beautiful all around me.
In beauty it is finished.

—Translated by Washington Matthews

NAVAJO

From a Sand Painting

There
the Earth Father high in the House of the Sky—
in his hands holds the sun,
in his hands holds the moon,
in his heart holds the earth.

There
the Earth Father high above the rainbow he stands—
from the sun in his hands
comes the light of all things;
from the moon comes the dreams;
from his heart comes the life of all things,
from his feet comes the joy.

The sun and the moon
in his hands send the rain,
the rainbow the kiss of the sun and the rain,
the smile of the sky.

The sun and the moon and the sky,
the Earth Father,
the Earth Mother;
the clouds and the rain brothers,
Elder Brothers,
hold the prayer plumes for man,
wave the prayer plumes for man,
wave the prayer plumes for man.

Let us dance in our joy, let us sing,
to our Brothers, our Brothers Above,
Elder Brothers
in the House of the Sky.

—*Translated by Ina Sizer Cassidy*

NAVAJO

The War God's Horse Song

I am the Turquoise Woman's son.
On top of Belted Mountain
Beautiful horses—slim like a weasel!
My horse has a hoof like striped agate;
His fetlock is like a fine eagle plume;
His legs are like quick lightning.
My horse's body is like an eagle-plumed arrow;
My horse has a tail like a trailing black cloud.

I put flexible goods on my horse's back;
The Little Holy Wind blows through his hair.

His mane is made of short rainbows.
My horse's ears are made of round corn.
My horse's eyes are made of big stars.
My horse's head is made of mixed waters
(From the holy waters—he never knows thirst).
My horse's teeth are made of white shell.
The long rainbow is in his mouth for a bridle,
      And with it I guide him.
When my horse neighs, different-colored horses
    follow.
When my horse neighs, different-colored sheep
    follow.
      I wealthy, because of him.

    Before me peaceful,
    Behind me peaceful,
    Under me peaceful,
    Over me peaceful,
    All around me peaceful—
    Peaceful voice when he neighs.
    I am everlasting and peaceful.
    I stand for my horse.

—Interpreted by Louis Watchman

NEZ PERCÉ

Chief Joseph's Surrender Speech

I am tired of fighting,
    Our chiefs are killed,
Looking Glass is dead,
    Toohulsote is dead.
The old men are all dead.
    It is the young men who say no and yes.
He who led the young men is dead.
    It is cold and we have no blankets.
The little children are freezing to death.
    My people, some of them, have run away to the
        hills.
No one knows where they are—
    Perhaps they are freezing to death.
I want to have time to look for my children
    and see how many of them I can find.
Maybe I shall find them among the dead.
    Hear me, my chiefs, I am tired,
My heart is sad and sick.
    From where the sun now stands
I will fight no more forever.

—Translated by Herbert Spinden

NEZ PERCÉ

Smohalla Speaks

You ask me to plow the ground!
    Shall I take a knife and tear my mother's bosom?
Then when I die she will not take me to her bosom to
        rest.

You ask me to dig for stone!
    Shall I dig under her skin for her bones?
Then when I die I can not enter her body to be born
        again.

    You ask me to cut grass and make hay and sell it,
And be rich like white men!
    But how dare I cut off my mother's hair?

It is a bad law and my people can not obey it.
    I want my people to stay with me here.
All the dead men will come to life again.
    Their spirits will come to their bodies again.
We must wait here in the homes of our fathers and
        be ready
    To meet them in the bosom of our mother.

—*Translated by James Mooney*

OJIBWAY

Song of a Man About to Die in a Strange Land

If I die here
In a strange land,
If I die
In a land not my own,
Nevertheless, the thunder
The rolling thunder
Will take me home.

If I die here, the wind,
The wind rushing over the prairie
The wind will take me home.

The wind and the thunder,
They are the same everywhere,
What does it matter, then
If I die here in a strange land?

—Reexpressed by Mary Austin

PAIUTE

In the Beginning

In the beginning water was
  everywhere
Then the buzzard lifted and the sky
  and the water ran to the west and
   made the ocean.
Then the buzzard made the trees,
  the plants, and all the tribes, and
   all the animals.
And the grizzly, the badger, and the
  gopher,
fearing that the water would come
  back, made the mountains with
   their hands.

PASSAMAQUODDY

Star Song

We are the singing stars,
We sing with our light.
We are the birds of fire,
Through the heavens we take our flight.

Our light is as a star,
Making a road for spirits.

Among us are three hunters
Forever chasing a bear.
There never was a time
When they three were not hunting.

We look down upon the mountains.

*—Translated by Charles Godfrey Leland
and John Dyneley Prince*

PLAINS CREE

Another Happening Was . . .

another happening was
this Blackfoot got suspicious about some man
—he's fucking you—he says
—o no—
—yes he is he's fucking you. Tomorrow you go
to the great sand-hill.—
And the next dawn he said—You, put on
your clothes; go out
and for the last time look
at the holy sun. Which
do you want, death
or that I cut off your nose?—
—Cut off my nose—she said.
He cut off her nose.

—*Translated by Armand Schwerner*

S. B. [Winnebago]

Peyote Vision

   I

 tried drinking coffee
     i would spill it
 sleeping
would see great snakes
   would cry out & get up
   raise my cover & look around
   had someone called me?
when the wind blew
    i heard singing
 people were spitting
 loudly i couldn't sleep
would see things happening in a distant country
ghosts on horseback drunk
five or six of them were on one horse
the song they sang was
"even i
  gotta die
    bye & bye
 so what's the use of anything
   i think"
later we used to sing it as a drinking song
lots of times

—*English version by Jerome Rothenberg
from the translation by Paul Radin*

TEWA

Song of the Sky Loom

O our Mother the Earth, O our Father the Sky,
Your children are we, and with tired backs
We bring you the gifts you love.
Then weave for us a garment of brightness;
May the warp be the white light of morning,
May the weft be the red light of evening,
May the fringes be the falling rain,
May the border be the standing rainbow.
Thus weave for us a garment of brightness,
That we may walk fittingly where birds sing,
That we may walk fittingly where grass is green,
O our Mother the Earth, O our Father the Sky.

—Translated by Herbert Joseph Spinden

ZUNI PRAYER

That their arms may be broken by the snow

That their arms may be broken by the snow,
In order that the land may be thus,
I have made my prayer sticks into living beings.

Following wherever the roads of the rain makers
     come out,
May the ice blanket spread out,
May the ice blanket cover the country;
All over the land
May the flesh of our earth mother
Crack open from the cold;
That your thoughts may bend to this,
That your words may be to this end;
For this with prayers I send you forth.

—Adapted by Ruth Bunzel

ZUNI

Sun Rays

See!
there across the sky
the Drawers-of-straight-Lines
flash their furrows of fire.
It is the Mind of the Father
on the borderland of Time,
the Father,
yearning,
yearning for his children
turned from the sky.

—Adapted by Ina Sizer Cassidy

ZUNI

The Coming of My People

In the dawning of the daylight,
in the beginning of the world,
from the womb of the Earth
my People came;
with the rumbling of eruptions,
with the trembling of the earthquakes
they were born.

In the blackness of midnight,
in the formlessness of Time
they had waited for the Word
to emerge;
in the stillness He had spoken,
in the silence they had heard Him
and obeyed.

—Adapted by Ina Sizer Cassidy

Lament of a Man For His Son

Son, my son!

I will go up to the mountain
And there I will light a fire
To the feet of my son's spirit,
And there lament him;
Saying,
O my son,
What is my life to me, now you are departed!

Son, my son,
In the deep earth
We laid you softly in a Chief's robe,
In a warrior's gear.
Surely there,
In the spirit land
Your deeds attend you
Surely,
The corn comes to the ear again!

But I, here,
I am the stalk that the seed-gatherers
Descrying empty, afar, left standing.
Son, my son!
What is my life to me, now you are departed!

—Adapted from the Amerindian by Mary Austin

Biographical Notes

ETEL ADNAN was born in Beirut, Lebanon in 1925. She has published a book, *Moonshine,* and her poems have appeared in *Where is Vietnam?* (Doubleday) and in *S. B. Gazette, Quixote* and other publications. "The Battle of Angels" was in manuscript.

ALTA was born in Reno, Nevada, in 1942. Her work has appeared in many magazines, and she edits for her own publishing concern, Shameless Hussy. "Thanksgiving" appeared in *The Whites of Their Eyes*(Seattle, 1970). She writes that she has Mandan ancestors.

JOHN ANGAIAK was born in Tununak, Alaska, in 1941. His poem "My Native Land, the Beautiful" appeared in the *Tundra Times,* Alaska.

ROBERT BACON was born in Bristol, Connecticut, in 1946. His work has appeared in *Dine Bas-Hani, Warpath,* and *Drums* (Indian newspapers). "Mister Scoutmaster" was in manuscript.

MARTHA WARREN BECKWITH (1871–1959) spent her childhood in Hawaii. She published *Hawaiian Mythology,* a comprehensive survey of island literature, and has translated *The Kumulipo,* a sacred creation myth, from which the extracts in this book are taken.

STEPHEN BERG was born in Philadelphia in 1934. He has published *The Daughters, Poems; Nothing in the Word;* co-translated *Clouded Sky;* and his poems have appeared in the *New Yorker, Poetry, New American Review, Tri-Quarterly,* and other magazines. His reexpression of "The Water of Kane" was in manuscript.

DUANE BIG EAGLE was born in Claremore, Oklahoma, in 1946. His work has appeared in *Florida Quarterly* and in *Quetzal.* "Bidato" first appeared as a broadside in 1971 published by the Cranium Press in San Francisco, California.

DOLLY BIRD was born in Minnesota in 1950. Her work has appeared in *Akwesasne Notes.* "Return to the Home We Made" was published in *Akwesasne Notes,* November–December 1970.

LEW (SHORT FEATHERS) BLOCKCOLSKI was born in Enid, Oklahoma, in 1943. His work has appeared in *The Galley Sail Review* and in *Steel-*

head. "Museum Exhibition" was published in *Akwesasne Notes,* November 1971.

ROBERT BLY was born in Minnesota, 1926. His work has appeared in the *Nation, Naked Poetry,* and *A Poetry Reading Against the Vietnam War.* "Anarchists Fainting" was published in *Harper's Magazine,* 1970.

MILLEN BRAND was born in Jersey City, New Jersey, 1906. His book of poems *Dry Summer in Provence* was published in 1966, and his work has appeared in *The New Yorker Book of Poems, Seeds of Liberation, New American Review.* "Behold Beloved" appeared in *Chelsea Magazine* and will be included in *Local Lives,* a book in preparation.

BESMILR BRIGHAM was born in Mississippi, 1923. She is the author of *Death of the Dancing Dolls;* and her work has appeared in *New Directions in Prose and Poetry* #21 and #23, and in many other magazines. "North from Tanyan" is taken from her book *Heaved from the Earth* (Alfred A. Knopf, 1971).

JOSEPH BRUCHAC was born in Saratoga Springs, New York, 1942. His work has appeared in *Chicago Review, Shenandoah, Hearse, The Nation,* and other magazines. "Indian Mountain" appeared in his book *Indian Mountain* (Ithaca House, 1971).

OLGA CABRAL was born in the West Indies, 1910. Her poems have appeared in the anthologies *Live Poetry* and *The Diamond Anthology.* "General Custer Enters Hell" comes from her book of poems *Tape Found in a Bottle* (Olivant Press, 1971).

GLADYS CARDIFF was born in Browning, Montana, 1942. Her work has appeared in *Inscape* and *Puget Soundings.* "Dragon Skate" was in manuscript.

EDMUND S. CARPENTER was born in 1922. "Men's Impotence" and "Who Comes" appeared in *Anerca* (J. M. Dent & Sons, Canada, 1959).

JAIME CARRERO was born in Mayagüez, Puerto Rico, in 1931. His work has appeared in *El Corno Emplumado-Mexico;* he has written seven plays, including *Pipo Subway No Sabe Reir,* which was shown in New York by Miriam Colon, and *Flag Inside.* He has also written two novels. His poem "Neo-Rican Jetliner" first appeared in *The San Juan Review,* April 1965.

HAYDEN CARRUTH was born in Waterbury, Connecticut, in 1921. He has published ten volumes of poetry, the most recent being *From Snow and Rock, From Chaos* (New Directions, Spring 1973). He is the editor of the anthology *The Voice That Is Great Within Us*

(Bantam). "At Dawn" appeared in his book *Nothing for Tigers* (Macmillan, 1965).

WILLIAM CHILDRESS was born in Hugo, Oklahoma, in 1933. His work has appeared in *Harpers, The Reporter, Good Housekeeping,* and other publications. "For an Indian Woman Dead in Childbirth" appeared in *America* and was included in his book *Lobo* (Barlenmir House, New York, 1972).

CARL CONCHA was born in Taos Pueblo, New Mexico. He has been a student at the Institute of American Indian Arts in Santa Fe. "The Spirit Dreams" appeared in the *South Dakota Review,* Vol. 7, No. 2, Summer 1969.

ROBERT J. CONLEY was born in Cushing, Oklahoma, 1940. His work has appeared in *Pembroke Magazine, Quetzal, Indian Voice Magazine,* and other publications. "We Wait" was in manuscript.

LEO CONNELLAN was born in Portland, Maine, in 1928. His work has appeared in the anthology *Where is Vietnam?* (Doubleday) and in the magazines *The Nation, Chelsea Review, New York Quarterly,* and other publications. "This Is A Stick-up" was in manuscript.

JEFFERSON DAVIS was born in Charlotte, North Carolina, in 1944. His work has appeared in *Sample Copy* (Chapel Hill, N. C., 1968) and in *Lillabulero* (#6 or #7). His poem "John Mason Gets Sassacus' Head" appeared in *Red Buffalo,* Summer 1921.

DR. NATHANIEL B. EMERSON (1839–1915) was born at Wailua, Oahu, of missionary parents. He was the translator of Malo's *Hawaiian Antiquities.* His most celebrated volume is *Unwritten Literature of Hawaii: The Sacred Songs of Hula* (1909). "The Water of Kane" is reexpressed from Emerson's translation.

JOSÉ-ANGEL FIGUEROA was born in Mayagüez, Puerto Rico, in 1946. His work has appeared in *Black Creation* and *The Daily World.* "a conversation w/ coca cola" appeared in *East 110th Street,* a book published by Broadside Press, 1971–1972.

DOUG FLAHERTY was born in Lowell, Massachusetts, in 1939. His work has appeared in *The New Yorker, The Nation,* and *The Quarterly Review of Literature.* "Snake Rite" was published in *Doones # 2,* 1970.

JOHN GILL was born in Chicago in 1924. His most recent book is *Gills's Blues,* published by the Crossing Press, Trumansburg, New York. He has also edited an anthology, *New American and Canadian Poetry* (Beacon Press, Boston, Mass.) "Something More Ghostly" was in manuscript.

DONALD DUANE GOVAN was born in Minot, North Dakota, in 1945. His work has appeared in *New Black Poetry, Ivory Tower Magazine, Minnesota Earth Journal.* The poem "Courage" appeared in the book *Fire Circled Rainbows* (Little Animal Press).

JOHN HAINES was born in Norfolk, Virginia, in 1924. His work has appeared in *The Hudson Review, Michigan Quarterly Review, Kayak,* and other publications. "The Traveler" appears in his book *Winter News* (Wesleyan Univ. Press, 1966).

WILLIAM HARMON was born in Concord, North Carolina, in 1938. He is the author of *Treasury Holiday* (Wesleyan Univ. Press, 1970), and his work appears in the anthology *Quickly Aging Here* (Doubleday, 1969). "Adaptation of Nahuatl Lament" was in manuscript.

MICHAEL S. HARPER was born in Brooklyn, New York. His books include *Dear John, Dear Coltrane; History As Apple Tree;* and *History Is Your Own Heartbeat* (University of Illinois Press, 1971), in which the poem "Prayer: Mt. Hood and Environs" appears.

J. C. HOLMAN lives in Tucson, Arizona. "Windsinger" appeared in *Chelsea 29.*

COLETTE INEZ was born in Brussels, Belgium, in 1931. She is the author of *The Woman Who Loved Worms* (Doubleday, 1972), and her work has appeared in *The Nation, Antioch Review, Beloit Poetry Journal, New York Quarterly,* and other magazines. The poem "Los Quatros Ijadas De Una Palabra" was in manuscript.

MANUEL JÁUREGUI was born in Denver, Colorado, in 1937. His poem "Untitled" appeared in *Sangre de la Raza* (May 20, 1970).

CHIRON KHANSHENDEL (BRONWEN E. ROSE) was born in Oakland, California, in 1948. Her work appears in *Speaking for Ourselves,* edited by Lillian Ladermand and Barbara Bradshaw (Scott-Foresman, 1971), and *Shadow of the Savage,* edited by Robert A. McGill, which is still in manuscript. She has published one collection of her own poems, *Songs for a Dancing Kachina* (Greenfield Review Press, Greenfield Center, New York). Her poem "Grandfather Pipestone Soul" appeared in *Warpath,* a magazine published by the United Native Americans, San Francisco.

LARRY LINDSAY KIMURA was born at Honoka'a, Hawaii, in 1946. "For Ha'Alo'U" appeared in *Hawaii Review,* December 1971.

ELIZABETH A. KONOPACKY was born in Marshfield, Wisconsin, in 1947. Her work has appeared in the magazine *Impersonal Circus* (University of Wisconsin). "Indian Tutoring Collage" appeared in *Poet* magazine.

PHILIP LEGLER was born in Dayton, Ohio, in 1928. He is the author of *A Change of View* and *The Intruder,* both collections of his poems. His work has appeared in *Poetry, The Nation, Quarterly Review of Literature,* and other magazines. "Campos Santo" was in manuscript.

JUNE LEIVAS was born in Parker, Arizona, in 1950. She is a member of the Chemehuevi Tribe. Her poem "No Indians Here" appeared in the *UCLA American Indian Culture Center Journal.*

MERIDEL LE SUEUR was born in Iowa in 1900. She is the author of *North Star Country, Salute to Spring,* and *The Crusaders.* Her work has appeared in *Poetry, Prairie Schooner, South Dakota Review,* and other magazines. Her poem "I Light Your Streets" was in manuscript.

GABRIEL O. LOPEZ was born in Albuquerque, New Mexico. His poem "Doing Time" appeared in the newspaper *El Grito del Norte.*

HOWARD MCCORD was born in El Paso, Texas, in 1932. His books include *The Diary of a Lost Girl, Maps and Gnomonology: A Handbook of Systems.* His work has appeared in *Partisan Review, Iowa Review, Kamadhenu.* "A Day's Journey with Geoffrey Young" appeared in his book *Fables and Transfigurations* (Kayak Books, 1967). He co-authored with Walter Lowenfels the prose book, "The Life of Fraenkel's Death" (Washington State University Press, 1970).

THOMAS MCGRATH was born in Sheldon, North Dakota, in 1916. His poems have appeared in *Poetry, The Nation,* and *Dacotah Territory,* and a number of books of poetry. "Letter to an Imaginary Friend" is from his book of the same name, published by Swallow Press, Spring 1970.

CARMEN M. MARTINEZ lives in New York. Her poems have appeared in *What's Happening, The Me Nobody Knows,* and *phat mama.* "ugliness #5" was in manuscript.

RAMÓN MARTINEZ was born in Albuquerque, New Mexico, in 1955. He is a high school senior, and "Cow Comes Home" is his first published poem. He has studied writing at summer Communicative and Creative Arts workshops at the University of Arizona.

JOHN MILTON was born in Anoka, Minnesota, in 1924. His work has appeared in *The Loving Hawk, This Lonely House,* and in *Poetry North.* "El Turista en El Pueblo" appeared in the book *The Tree of Bones* (Verb publications, Denver, 1965).

N. SCOTT MOMADAY was born in Lawton, Oklahoma, in 1934. His books include the novel *House Made of Dawn* (which won a 1969 Pulitzer Prize), and *The Way to Rainy Mountain;* and his poems have appeared in *Ramparts.* His poem "Earth and I Gave You Turquoise" appeared in the *New Mexico Quarterly.*

ROBERT NELSON MOORE, JR., was born in Chicago in 1943. His work has appeared in *Wormwood Review, Nola Express, The Smith.* "An Offering to the Dawn Princess" was in manuscript.

MICHAEL MOOS was born in Fargo, North Dakota, in 1949. His work has appeared in *Crazy Horse* and in *Dacotah Territory,* from which the poem "Cheyenne River Valley" was taken.

DUANE NIATUM was born in Seattle, Washington, in 1938. His work has appeared in *The New York Quarterly* and *Prairie Schooner,* and he is author of *After The Death of An Elder Klallam & Other Poems.* The poem "Ascending Red Cedar Moon" was in manuscript.

MICHAEL R. NICHOLAS was born in Mobile, Alabama, in 1941. His work has appeared in *Mele,* Nos. 4, 6, 7, and 8, and in *Journal of Black Poetry,* Vol. 1, No. 9. "The Unbuilt Sand Castles of Hawaii" appeared in his book *Watermelons into Wine* (Univ. of Hawaii, May 1968).

CHARLES OLSON (1910–1971) was born in Worcester, Massachusetts. His books include *Maximus Poems IV, V, VI; The Maximus Poems:* Volume Three (forthcoming); *Archaeologist of Morning;* and *The Maximus Poems* (Jargon/Corinth Books, New York, 1960) in which "Maximus, to Gloucester, Letter 157" appears.

SIMON J. ORTIZ was born in Albuquerque, New Mexico, in 1941. His work has appeared in *Alcheringa, New Mexico Quarterly,* and *Pembroke Magazine.* "War Poem" was in manuscript.

RONALD OVERTON was born on Long Island, New York, in 1943. His work has appeared in *Sumac, Hanging Loose, Epos,* and a number of other magazines. His "Found Poems" appeared in *NEW: American and Canadian Poetry* #11, December 1969.

GUY OWEN was born in Clarkton, North Carolina, in 1925. His most recent novels are *Journey for Joede,* nominated for the Pulitzer Prize, and *The Flim-Flam Man and the Apprentice* (Griffin). His poem "Who Speaks For The Red Man?" appeared in *Pembroke Magazine,* 1970.

HAIHAI PAWO PAWO (White Bird) was born at the Turtle Mountain Indian Reservation, Belcourt, North Dakota. Her work has appeared in *Akwesasne Notes, New Breed News,* and other Indian newspapers. "Alcatraz . . . Lives!!" appeared in *Akwesasne Notes* and *New Breed News*. She writes: "(I write only for the purpose of trying to salve a lagging and very tired spirit). Though I am a Ojibwa, I was given this name through my work with the prison groups for the nation of the Nez Perce."

MARGE PIERCY was born in Detroit in 1936. Her books include the novels *Breaking Camp* and *Going Down Fast*, and two books of poems: *Dance the Eagle to Sleep*, and *Hard Loving* (Wesleyan Univ. Press, 1969), in the last of which her poem "Curse of the earth magician on a metal land" appears.

DAVID RAY was born in Sapulpa, Oklahoma, in 1932. His work has appeared in *The Atlantic Monthly, The Paris Review,* and *The London Magazine*. His poem "The Indians Near Red Lake" was in manuscript.

FRED RED CLOUD was born in Bennetts Corners, Ohio, in 1928. He is of Seneca descent (Iroquois). His work has appeared in *Prairie Schooner, Wisconsin Review,* and *Voices International*. A book, *Poems and Legends of the Red Man,* is in process. "White Man Says to Me" appeared in *Akwesasne Notes*.

BENJAMIN H. ROGERS was born in Sioux City, Iowa, in 1949. His work has appeared in *Broadside Press, The Long View Journal,* and *Wascana Review* (Canadian). "The Man Above the Land" was in manuscript.

JEROME ROTHENBERG was born in New York City in 1931. His work has appeared in *Alcheringa: Ethnopoetics* ("first magazine of the world's tribal poetries"), which he co-edits with Dennis Tedlock, and in *The New Open Poetry*. His books include *Poems for the Game of Silence; Shaking the Pumpkin* (Doubleday, 1972); *Technicians of the Sacred* (Doubleday, 1968), in the latter two of which the poems "Peyote Vision" and "The Dead Hunter" appeared.

MICHAEL RUMAKER was born in Philadelphia in 1932. His work has appeared in *The Nation, Red Book, ER, Cosmopolitan,* and other magazines; he is the author of *The Butterfly* (a novel), and *Gringos and Other Stories*. "Poem" appeared in *Evergreen Review, #35.*

NORMAN H. RUSSELL was born in Big Stone Gap, Virginia, in 1921. He is the author of *indian thoughts: the small songs of god,* and his work has appeared in *Poetry Northwest, South Dakota Review,* and other magazines. "anna wauneka comes to my hogan" appeared in *Midwest Quarterly,* Winter 1970.

LUIS OMAR SALINAS was born in Robstown, Texas, in 1937. His work has appeared in *Aztlan,* a book by Valdez and Stiener; and in *Speaking for Ourselves* by Federman. "Aztec Angel" is from *Crazy Gypsy.*

RICARDO SÁNCHEZ was born in El Paso, Tejas, Aztlan, in 1941. His books include: *Canto y Grito Mi Liberacion* (Mictla Publications); *Points of Departure* (John Wiley & Sons, Inc.); *Obras* (Quetzl Press). His work has been published in *El Grito, Quinto Sol Publications,* and others. "Introduction to Abelardo" comes from *Los Cuatro* (Barrio Press, Denver, Colo., 1972), edited by Ricardo Sánchez.

ROBERTO SANDOVAL was born in Taos, New Mexico, in 1950. His work has appeared in *Puerto del Sol* (New Mexico State Press, 1972). "Tight Mouth" was in manuscript.

RUTH LISA SCHECHTER was born in Boston, Massachusetts. Her work has appeared in *New York Quarterly, Prairie Schooner, Beloit Poetry Journal,* and many other magazines. Her books include *Near the Wall of Lion Shadows; Movable Parts; Poetry the Healer;* and *Suddenly Thunder* (Barlenmir House, New York City, 1972), in which her poem "Along Missouri" appears.

ARMAND SCHWERNER was born in Antwerp, Belgium, in 1927. His books include: *The Tablets I–XV* (Grossman, New York); *Seaweed* (Black Sparrow, Los Angeles); *The Light Fall* (Hawks Well, New York). His reexpressions of Hawaiian poems were in manuscript.

BOOTS SIREECH was born at Fort Duquesne, Utah, in 1952. He belongs to the Ute tribe. His work has appeared in *Luchip Spearhead,* a publication of the Lutheran Church. "My Son" appeared in his book *Ten Poems, The Blue Cloud Quarterly,* Vol. IV, No. 3, 1969 (Benedictine Abbey, Marvin, South Dakota).

RAY SMITH was born in Minneapolis, Minnesota, in 1915. His work has appeared in *Poetry, University Review, Southern Humanities Review,* and in the anthology *Poets of Today.* "A Fragment for Last Pony of the Dacotah" appeared in *South Dakota Review,* Vol. 3, No. 1 (Autumn 1965), under the title "On the Little Bighorn."

WILLIAM STAFFORD was born in Hutchinson, Kansas, in 1914. His books include: *Traveling Through the Dark, The Rescued Year, Allegiances* (poetry collections, Harper & Row). His work has appeared in *Atlantic, Harper's, New Yorker, Poetry.* "People Who Went by in Winter" appeared in *Field* (Oberlin College).

HUGO STANCHI was born in Buenos Aires, Argentina, in 1941. "To Buss's Grandma" was in manuscript.

GENEVIEVE TAGGARD (1894–1948) was born in Waitsburg, Washington, and grew up in Honolulu, attending Oahu College. She was an editor and the author of a number of books of poetry and her work has appeared in many anthologies. "The Luau" comes from her book *Origin Hawaii* (David Angus, Honolulu, 1947).

PIRI THOMAS was born in Harlem Hospital, New York, in 1928. He is the author of the novel *Down These Mean Streets* and *Saviour Saviour Hold My Hand* (Doubleday, 1972), in which his poem "A First Night in El Sing Sing Prison" appears.

QUINCY TROUPE was born in New York City, 1943. His work has appeared in *New Black Voices* (New American Library); *Black Spirits* (Random House); *Black World;* and in *Embryo* (Barlenmir House, Fall 1972), from which his poem "Red Bone Pot Lunch" is taken.

ROBERT VARGAS was born in Managua, Nicaragua, in 1941. His work appears in *Litteratura Chicana,* Texto-Contexto (Joseph Sommers-Shuler) and in *Aztlan* (Valdez-Steiner, Vintage, 1972). His books include *Hispa America* (published in Argentina) and *Primeros Cantos,* a book of poems published by Ediciones "Pochoche," 1972. "Blame It on the Reds" appeared in the book *To Serve the Devil* (Vintage, 1971).

CHARLIE VERMONT was born in New York City in 1945. His work has appeared in *Io, Big Sky, The Paris Review,* and in his book *Two Women* (published by Angel Hair). "Dream" was in manuscript.

JUAN VILLEGAS was born in Harlem in 1954. He is the author of the book *Street Verse'n Some Righteousness* (Manna House Workshops, Inc., 1972), in which "WSLUM Presents" appears.

MARK VINZ was born in North Dakota in 1942. His work has appeared in *The Nation, The South Dakota Review, The Lamp in the Spine, American Dialog.* "Dakota Death Song" appeared in manuscript.

GERALD ROBERT VIZENOR was born in Minneapolis, Minnesota, in 1934. His work has appeared in the following anthologies: *The Way: An Anthology of American Indian Literature,; The Pursuit of Poetry,* and *An American Indian Anthology.* "Haiku" appeared in his books *Empty Swings* (Nodin Press, Minneapolis, 1967) and in *Seventeen Chirps* (Nodin Press, Minneapolis, 1964).

MARNIE WALSH was born in Black Hills, South Dakota. "John Knew the Crow" was published in *Dacotah Territory,* February 1972.

WILLIAM WANTLING was born in Peoria, Illinois, in 1933. His work has appeared in over 300 "little," avant-garde and underground publications—primarily in England and Wales. "Initiation" appeared in *Nola Express*, 1970.

RAMONA WEEKS was born in Phoenix, Arizona, in 1934. Her work has appeared in *Yale Review, Kenyon Review, Sewanee Review;* in *A Part of Space: Ten Texas Writers,* and *American Literary Anthology No. 2* (Random House, 1970). "An Aleutian Illusion" appeared in *Descant*, Summer 1970.

JAMES WELCH was born in Browning, Montana, 1940, on the Blackfoot Indian Reservation. His poems have appeared in *Harper's Bazaar, The New Yorker, Poetry, Hearse,* and *Kayak.* "Getting Things Straight" appeared in *Hearse # 14.*

TOM WHITECLOUD was born in California (died in 1971). He was part Ojibway. "Thief" appeared in *Akwesasne Notes* (volume #3, 4).

ANNA WHITE FEATHER was born in Buffalo, New York, in 1938. Her work has appeared in *Io, Dharma Continuum, Newt, Roughshod Animals* and *Amphora.* "Near Tassajara Bon Owl—to be sung" appeared in *Io—Earth Geography Booklet,* February 1972.

NANCY WILLARD was born in 1936. Her work has appeared in *Esquire, Antioch Review, Audience.* She is the author of "19 Masks for a Naked Poet" (Kayak Press). "I can remember when there were trees" was in manuscript.

KEITH WILSON was born in Clovis, New Mexico, in 1927. His work has appeared in *Poetry, Tri-Quarterly, Prairie Schooner;* and he is the author of *Homestead; Mid Watch; The Old Man and Others;* and *Graves Registry & Other Poems* (Grove Press, New York, 1969), in which his poem "Koyemsi" appeared.

PHILIP WOFFORD was born in Van Buren, Arkansas, in 1935. He is the author of *Grand Canyon Search Ceremony* (Barlenmir House, New York City, 1972). His work has appeared in *El Corno Emplumado.* "The Old and the Young Dance Separately" was in manuscript.

RAY YOUNG BEAR was born in 1950 in Tama, Iowa. His work has appeared in the *The Phoenix, Edge* and *Seneca Review.* "Through Lifetime" appeared in *South Dakota Review,* Summer 1971.

About the Editor

WALTER LOWENFELS, a native New Yorker, was one of the expatriate poets in the Paris of the twenties and thirties when Henry Miller called him "probably *the* poet of the age." Then he stopped writing, returned to the United States, and only resumed publishing in the past decade.

In addition to his own poems, Lowenfels is the author of *Walt Whitman's Civil War* and several popular anthologies including *Poets of Today, Where Is Vietnam?, In a Time of Revolution* and *The Writing on the Wall.* He is the author of a prose work: *To an Imaginary Daughter,* and has the following volumes of poetry in print: *Some Deaths, Land of Roseberries, Translations from Scorpius,* a prose book, *The Poetry of My Politics,* and *The Portable Walter,* a selection of his own prose and verse, edited by Robert Gover. His most recent publications are *Found Poems,* published on his seventy-fifth birthday, and *The Revolution Is to Be Human* (1973).

He lives with his wife, Lillian, in Peekskill, New York. They have four daughters and twelve grandchildren.

V-158   AUDEN, W. H. and C. ISHERWOOD   *Two Great Plays: The Dog Beneath the Skin and The Ascent of F6*

V-601   AUDEN, W. H. and PAUL TAYLOR (trans.)   *The Elder Edda*

V-673   BECK, JULIAN and JUDITH MALINA   *Paradise Now*

V-342   BECKSON, KARL (ed.)   *Aesthetes and Decadents of the 1890's*

V-271   BEDIER, JOSEPH   *Tristan and Iseult*

V-321   BOLT, ROBERT   *A Man for All Seasons*

V-21   BOWEN, ELIZABETH   *The Death of the Heart*

V-48   BOWEN, ELIZABETH   *The House in Paris*

V-294   BRADBURY, RAY   *The Vintage Bradbury*

V-670   BRECHT, BERTOLT   *Collected Works,* Vol. I

V-207   CAMUS, ALBERT   *Caligula & 3 Other Plays*

V-2   CAMUS, ALBERT   *The Stranger*

V-223   CAMUS, ALBERT   *The Fall*

V-245   CAMUS, ALBERT   *The Possessed, a play*

V-281   CAMUS, ALBERT   *Exile and the Kingdom*

V-626   CAMUS, ALBERT   *Lyrical and Critical Essays*

V-135   CAPOTE, TRUMAN   *Other Voices, Other Rooms*

V-148   CAPOTE, TRUMAN   *The Muses Are Heard*

V-643   CARLISLE, OLGA   *Poets on Streetcorners: Portraits of Fifteen Russian Poets*

V-28   CATHER, WILLA   *Five Stories*

V-200   CATHER, WILLA   *My Mortal Enemy*

V-679   CATHER, WILLA   *Death Comes for the Archbishop*

V-680   CATHER, WILLA   *Shadows on the Rock*

V-140   CERF, BENNETT (ed.)   *Famous Ghost Stories*

V-203   CERF, BENNETT (ed.)   *Four Contemporary American Plays*

V-127   CERF, BENNETT (ed.)   *Great Modern Short Stories*

V-326   CERF, CHRISTOPHER (ed)   *The Vintage Anthology of Science Fantasy*

V-293   CHAUCER, GEOFFREY   *The Canterbury Tales,* a prose version in Modern English

V-142   CHAUCER, GEOFFREY   *Troilus and Cressida*

V-723   CHERNYSHEVSKY, N. G.   *What Is to Be Done?*

V-146   CLARK, WALTER VAN T.   *The Ox-Bow Incident*

V-589   CLIFTON, LUCILLE   *Good Times*

V-173   CONFUCIUS (trans. by A. Waley)   *Analects*

V-155   CONRAD, JOSEPH   *Three Great Tales: The Nigger of the Narcissus, Heart of Darkness, Youth*

V-10   CRANE, STEPHEN   *Stories and Tales*

V-531   CRUZ, VICTOR HERNANDEZ   *Snaps: Poems*

V-205   DINESEN, ISAK   *Winter's Tales*

V-721   DOSTOYEVSKY, FYODOR   *Crime and Punishment*

V-722   DOSTOYEVSKY, FYODOR   *The Brothers Karamazov*

V-188   ESCHENBACH, WOLFRAM VON   *Parzival*

V-254   FAULKNER, WILLIAM   *As I Lay Dying*

V-139   FAULKNER, WILLIAM   *The Hamlet*

V-282   FAULKNER, WILLIAM   *The Mansion*

V-339   FAULKNER, WILLIAM   *The Reivers*

V-381   FAULKNER, WILLIAM   *Sanctuary*

V-5   FAULKNER, WILLIAM   *The Sound and the Fury*

V-184   FAULKNER, WILLIAM   *The Town*

V-351   FAULKNER, WILLIAM   *The Unvanquished*

V-262   FAULKNER, WILLIAM   *The Wild Palms*

V-149 FAULKNER, WILLIAM *Three Famous Short Novels: Spotted Horses, Old Man, The Bear*

V-130 FIELDING, HENRY *Tom Jones*

V-45 FORD, FORD MADOX *The Good Soldier*

V-187 FORSTER, E. M. *A Room With a View*

V-7 FORSTER, E. M. *Howards End*

V-40 FORSTER, E. M. *The Longest Journey*

V-61 FORSTER, E. M. *Where Angels Fear to Tread*

V-219 FRISCH, MAX *I'm Not Stiller*

V-8 GIDE, ANDRE *The Immoralist*

V-96 GIDE, ANDRE *Lafcadio's Adventures*

V-27 GIDE, ANDRE *Strait Is the Gate*

V-66 GIDE, ANDRE *Two Legends: Oedipus and Theseus*

V-656 GILBERT, CREIGHTON *Complete Poems and Selected Letters of Michelangelo*

V-473 GOODMAN, PAUL *Adam and His Works: Collected Stories of Paul Goodman*

V-402 GOODMAN, PAUL *Hawkweed*

V-654 GOODMAN, PAUL *Homespun of Oatmeal Gray*

V-300 GRASS, GUNTER *The Tin Drum*

V-425 GRAVES, ROBERT *Claudius the God*

V-182 GRAVES, ROBERT *I, Claudius*

V-717 GUERNEY, B. G. (ed.) *An Anthology of Russian Literature in the Soviet Period*

V-255 HAMMETT, DASHIELL *The Maltese Falcon* and *The Thin Man*

V-15 HAWTHORNE, NATHANIEL *Short Stories*

V-476 HOROWITZ, ISRAEL *First Season*

V-489 HOROVITZ, I. AND T. MCNALLY AND L. MELFI *Morning, Noon and Night*

V-305 HUMPHREY, WILLIAM *Home from the Hill*

V-727 ILF AND PETROV *The Twelves Chairs*

V-295 JEFFERS, ROBINSON *Selected Poems*

V-380 JOYCE, JAMES *Ulysses*

V-484 KAFKA, FRANZ *The Trial*

V-683 KAUFMANN, WALTER *Cain and Other Poems*

V-536 KESSLER, LYLE *The Watering Place*

V-134 LAGERKVIST, PAR *Barabbas*

V-240 LAGERKVIST, PAR *The Sibyl*

V-23 LAWRENCE, D. H. *The Plumed Serpent*

V-71 LAWRENCE, D. H. *St. Mawr and The Man Who Died*

V-315 LEWIS, ANTHONY *Gideon's Trumpet*

V-553 LOWENFELS, WALTER (ed.) *In a Time of Revolution: Poems from Our Third World*

V-537 LUKE, PETER *Hadrian VII*

V-673 MALINA, JUDITH AND JULIAN BECK *Paradise Now*

V-136 MALRAUX, ANDRE *The Royal Way*

V-479 MALRAUX, ANDRE *Man's Fate*

V-180 MANN, THOMAS *Buddenbrooks*

V-3 MANN, THOMAS *Death in Venice and Seven Other Stories*

V-86 MANN, THOMAS *The Transposed Heads*

V-496 MANN, THOMAS *Confessions of Felix Krull, Confidence Man*

V-497 MANN, THOMAS *The Magic Mountain*

V-36 MANSFIELD, KATHERINE *Stories*

V-137 MAUGHAM, SOMERSET *Of Human Bondage*

V-78 MAXWELL, WILLIAM *The Folded Leaf*

V-91 MAXWELL, WILLIAM *They Came Like Swallows*

V-221 MAXWELL, WILLIAM *Time Will Darken It*

V-580 WILLIAMS, MARGARET (trans.) *The Pearl Poet*

V-489 McNALLY, T. AND I. HOROVITZ AND L. MELFI *Morning, Noon and Night*

V-562 McNALLY, TERENCE *Sweet Eros, Next and Other Plays*

V-489 MELFI, L., I. HOROVITZ, T. McNALLY *Morning, Noon and Night*

V-593 MERWIN W. S. (trans.) *The Song of Roland*

V-306 MICHENER, JAMES A. *Hawaii*

V-718 NABOKOV, V. (trans.) *The Song of Igor's Campaign*

V-29 O'CONNOR, FRANK *Stories*

V-49 O'HARA, JOHN *Butterfield 8*

V-276 O'NEILL, EUGENE *Six Short Plays*

V-18 O'NEILL, EUGENE *The Iceman Cometh*

V-165 O'NEILL, EUGENE *Three Plays: Desire Under the Elms, Strange Interlude and Mourning Become Electra*

V-125 O'NEILL, EUGENE JR. AND WHITNEY OATES (eds.) *Seven Famous Greek Plays*

V-586 PADGETT, RON AND DAVID SHAPIRO (eds.) *An Anthology of New York Poets*

V-478 PARONE, EDWARD (ed.) *Collision Course*

V-466 PLATH, SYLVIA *The Colossus and Other Poems*

V-594 PROUST, MARCEL *Swann's Way*

V-595 PROUST, MARCEL *Within A Budding Grove*

V-596 PROUST, MARCEL *The Guermantes Way*

V-597 PROUST, MARCEL *Cities of the Plain*

V-598 PROUST, MARCEL *The Captive*

V-599 PROUST, MARCEL *The Sweet Cheat Gone*

V-600 PROUST, MARCEL *The Past Recaptured*

V-714 PUSHKIN, ALEXANDER *The Captain's Daughter*

V-24 RANSOM, JOHN CROWE *Poems and Essays*

V-732 REEVE, F. (ed.) *Russian Plays, Vol. II*

V-297 RENAULT, MARY *The King Must Die*

V-564 RUDNIK, RAPHAEL *A Lesson From the Cyclops and Other Poems*

V-16 SARTRE, JEAN-PAUL *No Exit and Three Other Plays*

V-65 SARTRE, JEAN-PAUL *The Devil and the Good Lord and Two Other Plays*

V-238 SARTRE, JEAN-PAUL *The Condemned of Altona*

V-586 SHAPIRO, DAVID AND RON PADGETT (ed.) *An Anthology of New York Poets*

V-330 SHOLOKHOV, MIKHAIL *And Quiet Flows the Don*

V-331 SHOLOKHOV, MIKHAIL *The Don Flows Home to the Sea*

V-153 STEIN, GERTRUDE *Three Lives*

V-85 STEVENS, WALLACE *Poems*

V-141 STYRON, WILLIAM *The Long March*

V-63 SVEVO, ITALIO *Confessions of Zeno*

V-178 SYNGE, J. M. *Complete Plays*

V-601 TAYLOR, PAUL AND W. H. AUDEN (trans.) *The Elder Edda*

V-750 TERTZ, ABRAM *The Trial Begins and On Socialist Realism*

V-713 TOLSTOY, LEO *The Kreutzer Sonata*

V-202 TURGENEV, IVAN *Torrents of Spring*

V-711 TURGENEV, IVAN *The Vintage Turgenev Vol. I: Smoke, Fathers and Sons, First Love*

V-712 TURGENEV, IVAN *Vol. II: On The Eve, Rudin, A Quiet Spot, Diary of a Superfluous Man*

V-257 UPDIKE, JOHN *Olinger Stories: A Selection*

V-605 WILLIAMS, JOHN A. AND CHARLES F. HARRIS, (eds.) *Amistad 1*

V-660 WILLIAMS, JOHN A. AND CHARLES F. HARRIS, (eds.) *Amistad 2*

V-580 WILLIAMS, MARGARET (trans.) *The Pearl Poet*